Fearless Women

Fearless Women

Athletes, Explorers, Other Competitors

Jillian Hanson

RAINTREE
STECK-VAUGHN
RSVP PUBLISHERS

A Harcourt Company

Austin · New York
www.steck-vaughn.com

Published by Raintree Steck-Vaughn Publishers, an imprint of
Steck-Vaughn Company

CREATED IN ASSOCIATION WITH MEDIA PROJECTS INCORPORATED
C. Carter Smith, *Executive Editor*
Carter Smith III, *Managing Editor*
Jillian Hanson, *Principal Writer*
Ana Deboo, *Project Editor*
Bernard Schleifer, *Art Director*
John Kern, *Cover Design*
Karen Covington, *Production Editor*

RAINTREE STECK-VAUGHN PUBLISHERS STAFF
Walter Kossmann, *Publishing Director*
Kathy DeVico, *Editor*
Richard Dooley, *Design Project Manager*

Photos on front cover, clockwise from top left: Annie Smith Peck,
Gail Devers, Sonja Henie, Picabo Street

Photos on title page, top to bottom: Mildred Bruce, Wilma Rudolph,
Floretta McCutcheon, Annie Oakley

Acknowledgments listed on page 80 constitute part of this copyright page.

Library of Congress Cataloging-in-Publication Data
Hanson, Jillian.
   Fearless women: athletes, explorers, other competitors / Jillian Hanson.
     p.   cm.—(Remarkable women: past and present)
   Includes index.
   Summary: Presents brief biographical sketches of women known as athletes,
explorers, or adventurers, from Harriet Chalmers Adams and Michelle Akers
to Kristi Yamaguchi and Babe Didrikson Zaharias.
   ISBN 0-8172-5729-2
   1. Women athletes—Biography Dictionaries Juvenile literature. 2. Women
explorers—Biography Dictionaries Juvenile literature. 3. Women—Biography
Dictionaries Juvenile literature. [1. Athletes. 2. Explorers. 3. Women Biography.]
I. Title. II. Series: Remarkable women.
GV697.H346   2000
796'.092'2—dc21   99-30147
[B]   CIP
Printed and bound in the United States
1 2 3 4 5 6 7 8 9 0 LB 03 02 01 00 99

CONTENTS

INTRODUCTION

THE DRIVE TO EXCEL IS A VERY POWERFUL FORCE. AS YOU READ THIS book, you will marvel at the accomplishments of these women, each of whom wanted more than anything to go the fastest or farthest, to defy gravity, develop a difficult skill, or accomplish a combination of those things. Some of them play games—basketball, tennis, even chess—with rules and human opponents. Some of them take on nature itself. They climb mountains, cross oceans, trek through deserts, and soar thousands of feet above the ground in rickety airplanes. And all of them demand the very most from themselves.

Many of them glory in performing death-defying feats. The women who loved to fly, especially, were willing to face danger—and death often caught up with them. Balloonist Sophie Blanchard; the pilots Bessie Coleman, Amelia Earhart, and Amy Johnson; and aerial acrobat Lillian Leitzel all lost their lives doing what they loved most. Explorers often traveled alone into uncharted regions where no western woman had ever been seen. They faced tropical fevers, scorching deserts, or mountain avalanches. Both Mary Kingsley and Ida Pfeiffer made a point of meeting cannibal tribes, and Pfeiffer was even captured by a hostile queen. Mountaineers Annie Smith Peck and Fanny Bullock Workman developed a spirited rivalry, each braving the dangers of ice and altitude to reach a higher summit than the other.

The thrill of winning motivates many of these women. They train endlessly with coaches who help them fight their weaknesses and make the most of their strengths, so they can perform flawlessly in competition. Track-and-field athlete Jackie Joyner-Kersee focused her versatility and drive on learning the heptathlon—seven separate events—and she won Olympic gold three times. Runner and perfectionist Mary Decker Slaney spent so many hours training that she actually had to learn how to hold back before she really started winning. Tennis player Billie Jean King used her drive to win to help her make a feminist statement. She challenged an especially boastful male pro, Bobby Riggs, to play her. She won.

However, it isn't always necessary to take first place to be a winner. Rower Silken Laumann's leg was terribly injured just weeks before the Olympics. Refusing to miss the games, she ignored the advice of doctors and family and, amazingly, came in third in the race. Aimee Mullins, a runner who lost both her legs, competes in the Paralympics. She hasn't yet won a medal because so few people in her situation become athletes; her opponents always have an advantage. But she has set many records in the double-amputee class.

A highly competitive athlete is at her peak for a limited time. Many have brilliant careers, retire, and start new lives just when most people are embarking on their first careers. Gymnast Olga Korbut was a pixielike 17-year-old when she stunned the world with her acrobatics. She retired at age 21 and became a coach. The legendary Babe Didrikson Zaharias moved from one sport to another during her career. She played semi-professional basketball, then won Olympic medals in track, and *then* became America's top female golfer.

Most of these women share a love of physical exertion and adventure. Constance Applebee, Senda Berenson, and Mary Outerbridge all made a point of teaching their games to others. They introduced women's field hockey, basketball, and tennis respectively to the United States. And Applebee happily coached field hockey until she was 95 years old. Let these stories inspire you, fire you up to try out some adventure of your own. Maybe an Olympic medal is in your future, too. But even if it's not, you can still thrill to the feeling of pushing yourself to the limits, engaging in a friendly competition, and rejoicing in a well-deserved victory.

Photos top left Lillian Leitzel, bottom left Fanny Bullock Workman,
top right Mildred Didrikson Zaharias, bottom right Althea Gibson.

Harriet Chalmers Adams (1875–1937)
Explorer, writer

As a little girl Harriet Chalmers went on camping trips with her gold prospector father and learned to love travel and exploration. A native of Stockton, California, Chalmers received most of her education from private tutors because she traveled so much with her parents. In 1899 she married an engineer named Franklin Adams and accompanied him on surveys in Mexico, Central America, and South America.

These early adventures in her married life sparked Harriet Adams's interest in Spanish-speaking and Native American cultures. She became a writer and lecturer, and she traveled widely—often by herself—to gather material. In the course of her journeys, she sought out almost every aboriginal culture in North and South America and retraced the steps of Spanish and Portuguese explorers around the world, a project that took her to remote destinations in North Africa, Asia, and the South Sea Islands. Her articles and photographs appeared regularly in *National Geographic* magazine, and she often spoke at the National Geographic Society in Washington, D.C. She was a founder and the first president of the Society for Woman Geographers, an international organization that is still active. Adams was known for her generous encouragement of other female travelers and writers.

Delia Denning Akeley (1875–1970)
Explorer

Mary Lee Jobe Akeley (1886–1966)
Explorer

As the first and second wives of the naturalist and artist Carl Akeley, Delia and Mary Akeley both fell in love with the African continent while assisting their husband in his work there. Both went on to lead valuable careers as explorers, writers, and preservationists.

Delia Denning, a Wisconsin native, met Carl Akeley when he was working for the Milwaukee Art Museum. They married in 1902 and traveled to Kenya three years later to collect plant and animal specimens for his museum exhibits. When Carl left her for another woman—Mary Jobe—in 1923, Delia went on to pursue her own projects. She traveled to the Belgian Congo (now known as the Democratic Republic of the Congo) and lived with the Pygmy tribe for several months so that she could study their culture and lifestyle. Upon her return home to America, Delia Akeley chronicled her African adventures in books such as *Jungle Portraits* (1930) and in assorted articles.

Delia Denning Akeley

The Ohio-born Mary Jobe started her career as an English professor at Hunter College in New York City. During a series of trips to the Northwest Territories of Canada, she became an explorer and skilled mountain climber. She married Carl Akeley in 1924, shortly after his divorce from Delia. In 1926 she accompanied him to Africa on an expedition to study gorillas. When he died of a fever later that year, she took over the expedition. King Albert of Belgium awarded her the Cross of the Knight in 1928 in recognition of her work. In the decades that followed, she became active in the growing movement to save African cultures and wildlife. She also wrote several books, among them *Restless Jungle* (1936).

Michelle Akers (1966–)
Soccer player

FROM THE TIME SHE WAS A TEENAGER IN SEATTLE, Washington, Michelle Akers was an accomplished athlete and a star on the soccer field. As a college student at the University of Central Florida, Akers was named all-American four years in a row, an uncommon achievement. She joined the U.S. national women's soccer team in 1985 and supported herself for several years by playing professionally in Europe. In 1991 she helped lead the American team to victory in the first women's world championship soccer tournament in China, during which she scored a record five goals in one match.

That year, however, Akers's health began to fail, and she was eventually diagnosed with a disease called chronic fatigue syndrome. After fighting debilitating exhaustion and a host of other symptoms, she was able to regain much of her stamina. She made a stunning comeback in the 1996 summer Olympics, leading her team to a gold medal. Akers is considered one of the world's greatest players. Like so many women athletes, her dream is to play professionally in America. She was a member of the U.S. soccer team during the 1999 Women's World Cup, and many people believe that the team's celebrated victory will attract the financial support needed to make a professional league possible.

Constance Applebee (1873–1981)
Field hockey player

AMERICANS HAVE ENGLISHWOMAN CONSTANCE Applebee to thank for introducing field hockey to their country. After graduating from the British College of Physical Education in London, Applebee moved to the United States and enrolled at Harvard University's Summer School of Physical Education in 1901. When her teachers at Harvard mentioned playing musical chairs for exercise, Applebee retorted that in England musical chairs was a party game—field hockey was a sport. Soon afterward, a group of women gathered in a paved yard outside the Harvard gymnasium and played field hockey for the first time. Forced to improvise their equipment, they used ice hockey sticks.

"The Apple," as she was known, became the director of health education at Bryn Mawr College in 1904 and coached their field hockey team for the next 63 years. For much of that time, she ran the Pocono Hockey Camp in Pennsylvania, and in 1922 she cofounded the United States Field Hockey Association (USFHA), which established official rules for the sport. She also edited and published the first American women's sports magazine, *Sportswomen*. Applebee was the living proof of her strong belief that field hockey promoted good physical and mental health—she coached until she was 95 and lived to be 107. She was inducted into the International Women's Sports Hall of Fame in 1991.

Yael Arad (1967–)
Judo champion

YAEL ARAD AND HER BROTHER YUVAL TOOK JUDO classes together when they were kids in Israel, and Yael discovered she was better at it than most of the boys. By age ten she was winning national championships in her age group. Arad interrupted her training for a mandatory tour of duty in the Israeli army when she was 18, but she was ready for the Olympic Games in Barcelona in 1992, the first year judo was included. Even the fact that she had had knee surgery four months earlier didn't slow her down.

In the finals for the half-middleweight title, Arad competed against France's Catherine Fleury. The match

The Olympic Games

Most top athletes share Yael Arad's dream of winning an Olympic medal. The famed Olympic Games are modeled on a sports festival that began in ancient Greece in the eighth century B.C.E. and continued until the Roman emperor Theodosius banned it in 393 C.E. Centuries later, a Frenchman, Baron Pierre de Coubertin, revived the idea to promote international goodwill. The first modern Olympics took place in April 1896. As in ancient Greece, they were held every four years thereafter, except during the world wars. Starting in 1924 a winter competition was added, and since 1992 the winter and summer games have occurred in alternate even years.

was a tie, and in a split decision the judges awarded Fleury the gold. A silver medal was good enough for the Israelis, though: This was their country's first Olympic medal ever, and Arad was a heroine. She dedicated her performance to the Israeli athletes slain by terrorists at the 1972 Olympics in Munich. Since the Barcelona games, she has established the Yael Arad Foundation to provide financial support to other Israeli athletes.

Isabelle Autissier (1956–)
Sailor

ISABELLE AUTISSIER GREW UP NEAR THE SEA, ON THE coast of Brittany in France. By the time she was 12, she had decided to sail solo around the world one day. She fulfilled that dream in 1991, when she was the first and only woman to enter the BOC Challenge (named after its sponsor, the British Oxygen Company). This grueling yacht race covers 27,000 miles (43,450 km), beginning and ending in Charleston, South Carolina. Autissier finished seventh in her class and returned home a heroine.

In 1994 Autissier sailed from New York to San Francisco around South America in just 62 days, five hours—two weeks faster than the standing record. Later that same year, she entered the BOC again and gained an early five-day lead, but she encountered difficulty on the stormy Indian Ocean. First she lost her 83-foot (25-m) mast. Then she was hit by a huge wave that rolled her yacht, causing irreparable damage. After four days of drifting in a sinking boat on rough seas, she was airlifted to safety. Determined not to let the ordeal end her career, she prepared for the 1998 BOC (now called the Around Alone), but once again she had to pull out of the race when her boat capsized. Autissier is also a marine scientist, and between races she teaches college courses in France.

Florence Finnian von Sass Baker (1841–1916)
Explorer

AS THE SECOND WIFE OF THE FAMOUS BRITISH explorer Samuel White Baker, Florence von Sass Baker was one of only a handful of 19th-century women to explore the African continent.

Although the Bakers worked as a team, Florence never received much recognition for her part in their extraordinary achievements, and little is known about her early life.

The couple met under strange circumstances when Florence was 17 years old. Legend has it that, while on a boar-hunting expedition in Hungary in 1859, the widower Samuel happened to pass by a Hungarian slave market just as the young woman was about to be sold. He bought her, and they married a year later. In 1861 they traveled to Ethiopia to search for the source of the Nile. Instead they found what is now known as Lake Albert and a waterfall they named Murchison Falls. The Bakers also spent four years in the southern Sudan, working to abolish the flourishing slave trade there. During her time in Africa, Florence faced every danger and hardship with aplomb, holding her own against the fierce jungle climate, tribal wars, and wild animals. In 1873 the devoted couple retired to Devonshire, England, where Samuel died 20 years later. Florence spent her last years with her stepchildren.

Iolanda Balas (1936–)
High jumper

IOLANDA BALAS IS CONSIDERED ONE OF THE GREATEST female high jumpers in track-and-field history. She leaped into the record books 14 times during her career, was the first woman to jump over six feet (1.8 m), and at her peak was undefeated for a decade—140 straight wins.

Balas, who was born in Timisoara, Romania, grew to be six feet tall by 1951, when she won the first of her 16 Romanian national titles. She took second place in the 1954 European championships. And although she came in a disappointing fifth at the 1956 Olympics in Melbourne, she soon began her winning streak. At the 1960 Olympic Games in Rome and four years later in Tokyo, she won the gold, becoming the only high jumper, male or female, ever to win twice at the Olympics.

Balas achieved her highest jump—6 feet, 3¼ inches (1.9 m)—in 1961, and that record stood for ten years. By 1967, however, she was increasingly plagued by injuries and lost a competition. She retired that year and married her coach, Ion Söter.

Jean Balukas (1959–)
Billiards player

POOL (OR BILLIARDS) HAS BEEN AROUND FOR centuries. It is mentioned in French and British historical records as early as the 1400s. But it is only in the last three or four decades that the game has attracted female players. This is because pool tables have traditionally been located in bars or private men's clubs, out of reach of all but a handful of women.

Jean Balukas was exposed to the game early—she started playing when she was five—because her father

was part-owner of a pool hall in Brooklyn, New York. Balukas began competing four years later and placed seventh in the women's U.S. Open. She went on to win the women's division world championship six times, the U.S. Open seven times, and was named Player of the Year five times. Balukas became the second woman and the youngest person ever to be inducted into the Billiard Congress of America Hall of Fame. She also excels at other sports, such as softball, golf, and tennis, and she is a top bowler in her Brooklyn league.

Gertrude Margaret Lowthian Bell (1868–1926)
Traveler, archaeologist, writer, mountain climber, government official

BORN INTO A WEALTHY FAMILY OF BRITISH industrialists, Gertrude Bell was the first woman ever to earn Oxford University's highest honors for the study of history. In her early 20s, she developed the passion for adventure, travel, and Middle Eastern

culture that would shape her life. She became a fearless adventurer, received by many of her hosts as if she were a man. She visited Jerusalem and Constantinople (now Istanbul), explored Syria and Persia (now Iran), and came to consider Iraq her home. She published several books about her travels and translated a volume of ancient Persian poetry into English. She made valuable contributions to maps and archaeological records of the Middle East. And she was a skilled mountain climber, famous for scaling unexplored peaks in the Swiss Alps.

During World War I, Bell was drafted as an agent of the British military intelligence. Government officials, who had previously viewed her adventures as eccentric and foolhardy, realized her familiarity with Arabian culture and the territory was of great strategic value. They sent her first to Egypt, then to Baghdad, where after the war she was appointed Oriental secretary to the British High Commission. Bell was instrumental in putting King Faisal, the leader of the Arab revolt, on the throne in the newly formed country of Iraq in 1921. Two years later she became director of the country's first national archaeological museum in Baghdad. Sadly, in the last years of her life, loneliness and depression plagued her. She died of an overdose of sleeping pills two days before her 58th birthday.

Joan Benoit Samuelson (1957–)
Long-distance runner

JOAN BENOIT'S FIRST LOVE WAS SKIING, BUT DURING her senior year in high school she broke her leg on the slopes and started running to regain her strength. Within a year she was competing in the Junior Olympics. In 1979 she began running marathons and won the most prestigious of them, the Boston Marathon, setting a new American women's record of 2 hours, 35 minutes, and 15 seconds. She coached track at Boston University from 1981 to 1983 before deciding to make competitive running her full-time career.

In 1983 Benoit won the Boston Marathon again, setting a new world record. The following year she won the gold medal in the first-ever women's Olympic marathon in Los Angeles, defeating Norway's Grete Waitz. After a number of other victories, she withdrew from racing for a few years to start a family with her husband, Scott Samuelson. Then she returned to competition with a solid fourth-place finish in the 1991 Boston Marathon. Although she still races, Benoit has begun to concentrate on promoting her sport. In 1998 she fulfilled a longtime ambition, organizing a ten-kilometer race near her hometown of Cape Elizabeth, Maine. The first annual Peoples Beach to Beacon attracted many world-class distance runners.

Senda Berenson (1868–1954)
Physical education instructor, basketball pioneer

LITHUANIAN-BORN SENDA BERENSON IMMIGRATED to America with her family when she was seven years old. She began her career in 1892, teaching physical education at Smith College in Northampton, Massachusetts. After reading about a new game called "basket ball," invented by James Naismith in nearby Springfield, she introduced it to her students. Her freshman and sophomore classes played their first match in 1893 and assisted her in adapting the rules for women.

Berenson emphasized a cooperative approach. Positioning and passing the ball from player to player were favored, rather than allowing one person to run it the full length of the court. Stealing the ball from a rival team member was not allowed, and players couldn't hold the ball for longer than three seconds or dribble more than three times. Berenson published *Line Basket Ball for Women* in 1901 and actively promoted the sport. It soon became popular at girls' schools throughout the country. Her rules remained the standard for women players until the 1960s.

Berenson married an English professor, Herbert Vaughn Abbott, in 1911 and retired from teaching ten years later to study art and music abroad. These were interests she shared with her brother, Bernard Berenson, a famous art critic. She spent the final years of her life in California. In 1984 she was inducted into the International Women's Sports Hall of Fame as well as the Naismith Memorial Basketball Hall of Fame.

Patricia Jane Berg (1918–)
Golfer

AS A CHILD, PATTY BERG QUARTERBACKED FOR HER neighborhood football team, ran track, played baseball, and competed as a speed skater in her hometown of Minneapolis, Minnesota. When she was 14 years old, she received her first set of golf clubs—and discovered her greatest passion.

It wasn't long before she was one of the country's top players. In 1938 Berg was named Outstanding Female Athlete of the Year by the Associated Press, an honor she would receive again in 1943 and 1955. She turned pro at the age of 22, even though there were only three professional tournaments for women

at the time. She went on to win an impressive 57 tournaments over all, including the first U.S. Women's National Open in 1946.

Berg enthusiastically promoted her sport. From 1949 to 1952, she served as the first president of the newly formed Ladies Professional Golf Association (LPGA). Throughout her career she made a practice of contributing time and money to charitable organizations. She toured the country conducting classes and giving clinics well into her 70s. Berg received numerous honors and was inducted into the LPGA Hall of Fame in 1951, the Professional Golfers' Association Hall of Fame in 1978, and the International Women's Sports Hall of Fame in 1980.

Juliana Berners (1388?–unknown)
Sportswoman, writer

IN 1496 AN ANTHOLOGY OF WRITINGS ABOUT hunting entitled *The Boke of St. Albans* was published in England, and a woman—Dame Juliana Berners—was credited with being its author. Scholars now think that several writers contributed to the book. However, most agree that Berners was responsible for at least one part, the *Treatise of Fishing With an Angle*, which is the first known work ever published on fly-fishing. Along with detailed instructions on how to construct a rod, hook, and line, she described how to tie flies, the insect-shaped lures used for fishing. She also included a conservationist's argument against overfishing.

> "...you must not be greedy in your catch, so as to take too many fish at one time, which you may do unthinkingly if you act according to these instructions, which will cause you to destroy your own sport and that of other men as well. And when you have caught a sufficient number of fish, you must covet no more for the time being. Also you must busy yourself in furthering the sport in every way that you can, and to destroy anything that tends to lower its morale."
>
> JULIANA BERNERS
> *Treatise of Fishing With an Angle*

As a young English noblewoman, Berners had delighted in hawking, hunting, and fishing, the popular recreations of her day. She was well-educated and known for her intelligence and beauty. It was in her later years that she began to write about her considerable sporting experiences. Some historical sources say that, by that time, she had withdrawn from society to become the prioress of the Sopwell Nunnery in Hertfordshire.

Isabella Lucy Bird Bishop (1831–1904)
Traveler, writer

AS A YOUNG WOMAN, ISABELLA BIRD VISITED Canada and the United States and wrote about her experiences in her successful first book, *The Englishwoman in America* (1856). However, despite her restless spirit and a prescription from her doctor to travel for her health, Bird would not leave home again until she was in her 40s. She was forced to remain in Yorkshire, England, nursing her sick parents.

After their deaths, with nothing to hold her back, Isabella eased her spinal pain and depression by setting off for distant ports and found that her health improved markedly once she left British soil. She

went alone to places where most Victorian ladies would never dare set foot, trekking boldly through Tibet, Japan, China, Persia, and the South Pacific. Bird chronicled her adventures and keen observations in several popular books, including *Unbeaten Tracks in Japan* (1880) and *Among the Tibetans* (1894). Her travels were briefly interrupted again after she married a Scottish doctor, John Bishop, in 1881. But Bishop died five years later, and she returned to her explorations.

In her later years, Bird traveled increasingly as a philanthropist and missionary. She established two hospitals in India in 1889 and, while in China five years later, founded an orphanage and three hospitals. In 1892 she was the first woman asked to address the Royal Geographical Society. A few months later, she was among the first 15 women offered membership in that distinguished, all-male organization. She continued traveling until her death at age 73.

Bonnie Blair (1964–)
Speed skater

AMERICAN SPEED SKATER BONNIE BLAIR COULD skate almost from the time she could walk. She won her first state championship race in Champaign, Illinois, at age seven and began training in earnest before she was a teenager. She set her sights on the Olympics but soon found she couldn't afford the expensive coaching and travel of an Olympic athlete. A decade-long fund-raising effort by the Champaign police department (they sold T-shirts and bumper stickers) helped finance the training she needed to be a world-class competitor. And Blair's subsequent career didn't disappoint the folks back home.

This small, cheerful woman, one of America's most popular athletes, has won five gold medals and a bronze—more winter Olympic medals than any other American to date. "Bonnie the Blur," as she became known, was also the first American woman to win gold medals in three consecutive Olympic Games: 1988, 1992, and 1994. She retired after winning the World Cup in 1995. However, she lives in Milwaukee, Wisconsin, where the U.S. skating team trains, and she still attends many speed-skating events, because her husband, David Cruikshank, is also a top speed skater. The couple had their first child, a son, in the summer of 1998.

Madeleine Sophie Blanchard (1778–1819)
Balloonist

SOPHIE BLANCHARD, THE WIFE OF A WELL-KNOWN French balloonist named Jean-Pierre Blanchard, became the first woman to pilot a flight when she went up alone in 1805. Madame Blanchard became well known for her night flights. It was said that she preferred sleeping in the sky to sleeping on the ground, because she had an intense fear of loud noises.

A tiny woman, with sharp, birdlike features, she became quite popular with the French public. After her husband died in 1809, she made her living entertaining spectators by ascending into the sky and launching fireworks attached to miniature parachutes from the basket of her balloon, all to the accompaniment of dramatic orchestral music. Napoleon even named her Official Aeronaut of the Empire. She died while performing at the Tivoli Gardens in Paris (a popular amusement park of the day that no longer exists). Blanchard's balloon caught fire, then crashed onto a nearby roof, and she was tumbled onto the street below.

Fanny Blankers-Koen (1918–)
Track-and-field athlete

FANNY BLANKERS-KOEN, AN OUTSTANDING TRACK-and-field athlete, was also a wife and mother of two at the peak of her career, something the press made much of when they nicknamed her "the Flying Dutch Housewife." As ridiculous as that may sound today, at the time it helped the world realize that women could excel in athletics and still maintain their femininity.

Born in Amsterdam, Fanny Koen began competing in 1935. She won many events over the next few years while training with coach Jan Blankers, whom she married in 1940. But she didn't win at the Olympics. She hadn't won a medal at the 1936 games in Berlin, and because of World War II, the next two Olympics were canceled. At the 1948 Olympic Games in London, many people assumed it was too late for the 30-year-old. As it turned out, she became the only woman ever to win four gold medals in track events at one Olympics—and she probably could have won more. Olympic rules restricted her to three individual events, so she chose the 100- and 200-meter sprints and the 80-meter hurdles, then ran on the 4x100-meter relay team. She would have had a chance of winning the high jump and the long jump, too.

Blankers-Koen continued to compete after this stunning Olympic performance, setting world records and collecting European championship medals and Dutch national titles until her retirement in 1955. She was inducted into the International Women's Sports Hall of Fame in 1980.

Arlene Blum (1945–)
Mountain climber

As a student at Reed College in Portland, Oregon, Arlene Blum combined her love of altitude climbing with her studies in chemistry by writing her undergraduate thesis about the volcanic gases on nearby Mount Hood. After being barred from joining a men's climbing team because of her sex, Blum led the first all-female expedition to the summit of Mount McKinley in Alaska in 1970. Then she began organizing a women's climb of the world's tenth-highest mountain, Annapurna in the Himalayas.

Mountaineer Scientist

While leading the adventurous life of an explorer, Arlene Blum did not abandon her interest in chemistry. She earned a Ph.D. from the University of California at Berkeley and became a teacher and researcher. As part of a scientific team, she discovered that a flame-retardant chemical known as Tris, which was being used to treat children's sleepwear, caused cancer. Tris was taken off the market in 1977.

Only four male teams had ever reached the summit of Annapurna by 1978, when Blum and her group set out. Two women reached the top on October 15th. Two days later, another pair attempted to get there but disappeared, probably in an avalanche. A grieving but determined Blum reminded those who blamed the accident on the fact that they were women that Annapurna, a mountain prone to avalanches and harsh weather, is dangerous to any climber.

Blum has continued to lead expeditions and teach climbing and leadership courses. For nine months in 1981 and 1982, she trekked the length of the Himalayan range, across Bhutan, Nepal, and India. She has also written articles for such magazines as *National Geographic* and *Science*.

Lady Anne Blunt (1837–1917)
Explorer

Lady Anne Noel, the granddaughter of the English poet Lord Byron, was raised primarily in continental Europe, where she became fluent in several languages. She was also a talented artist and musician and was fascinated by Arab culture. In 1869 she married the poet and diplomat Wilfrid Scawen Blunt. Together, they undertook a series of adventures in Arabia that made them famous.

Lady Anne didn't employ a caravan of servants, guides, and supplies like other English travelers of that era but traveled lightly, wearing Arab dress for convenience. She endured sandstorms, and ate locusts and hyena, while becoming the first western woman to explore the Nejd region in central Saudi Arabia. She was practical and level-headed in all her encounters. Her two books, *Bedouin Tribes of the Euphrates* (1879) and *A Pilgrimage to Nejd* (1881), became quite popular.

In 1882 the Blunts bought Sheykh Obeyd, a 37-acre (15-ha) estate in Egypt. They began to spend much of their time at this desert refuge, returning now and then to their home in Sussex, England. In 1906 Lady Anne separated amicably from her husband and resided almost exclusively in Egypt, adopting Arabic as her first language. She died in Cairo and was buried in a small graveyard just outside the city.

Louise Arner Boyd (1887–1972)
Arctic explorer, photographer

L OUISE BOYD, A SOCIALITE FROM SAN RAFAEL, California, saw the Arctic for the first time from a Norwegian cruise boat in 1924. Inspired by the cold beauty of the landscape, she chartered her own boat the next year. In 1928 she joined the search for the famous Arctic explorer, Roald Amundsen, who had disappeared in a plane crash.

After four months, Amundsen was given up for lost, but Boyd's career was launched. She had met explorers and scientists from all over the world and shot several thousand photographs. Luckily, her wealth—the Boyd family money was made during the Gold Rush—allowed her to finance her career. During her next four expeditions, Boyd became an accomplished photographer, recording the terrain and plant life of East Greenland's fjords. Her knowledge of Arctic geography led to her appointment as an adviser for the United States government during World War II.

Boyd retired to her California estate considerably less wealthy, but with enough money left to realize one more dream. In 1955, at age 68, she chartered a plane and became the first woman to fly over the North Pole.

Midge "Toughie" Brasuhn (left) takes a hit from a member of the Jersey Jolters.

often violent sport, which involved two, five-person teams racing around a small track and trying by any means possible to prevent each other from taking the lead. The public thronged to arenas or turned on their televisions to cheer for such idols as Midge Brasuhn.

Brasuhn, a native of St. Paul, Minnesota, was less than 5 feet (1.5 m) tall and as wholesome-looking as her Midwestern roots might suggest. But she was indomitable in the rink and became a huge celebrity. It was said that she had a terrible temper and no fear for her own safety, a reputation that earned her the nickname "Toughie." She started skating in the Transcontinental Roller Derby in 1941, and in 1950 she was voted one of the country's top ten women athletes by sportswriters. Brasuhn retired in Honolulu, Hawaii, in the 1960s. By then roller derby's heyday was nearly over, too; it ended in the early 1970s.

Midge "Toughie" Brasuhn (1923–1971)
Roller derby star

R OLLER DERBY, A FAST AND ROUGH GAME PLAYED on roller skates, became instantly popular in the United States when it was televised for the first time in 1948. Both men and women competed in the

Mildred Mary Bruce (1895–1990)
Driver, boater, aviator

M ILDRED BRUCE LOVED TO GO FAST. SHE BECAME the first woman in Britain ever to be charged with speeding when, in 1910, a policeman caught her doing 67 miles per hour (108 kph) on her brother's

motorcycle. She also loved cars—she raced at Monte Carlo and broke several speed and distance records.

Using her eminently respectable married name—the Honorable Mrs. Victor Bruce—she became known for antics such as driving across the Sahara or through Lapland. She raced motorboats, too. In 1929 she set a speed record for motorboating across the English Channel and back, as well as a record for traveling the farthest on the Atlantic Ocean in a 24-hour period.

Not surprisingly, as soon as she could get her hands on an airplane, she learned to fly. In 1930 she set a record for the longest solo journey by a female pilot, traveling from London to Japan. That same year she was arrested for flying circles around the Empire State Building in New York City. She also flew with an aerial circus and operated an air-ferry across the English Channel between Great Britain and France. At age 78 she was still test-driving cars for the Ford Motor Company. She published her autobiography, *Nine Lives Plus*, in 1977 and lived to be 94 years old.

Beryl Burton (1937–1996)
Bicyclist

A DOWN-TO-EARTH WOMAN WHO SHUNNED publicity and worked on a rhubarb farm in her native Yorkshire, England, Beryl Burton was one of the world's greatest cyclists, male or female. She started riding at age 15 and over the course of her career, won more than 80 British titles and seven world championships. In 1959 she earned the women's British Best All-Rounder title for being the fastest woman racer in three distances: 25, 50, and 100 miles (40, 80, and 160 km). She held the All-Rounder title for the next 24 years.

At the peak of Burton's career, she regularly beat top male cyclists. In 1967 she set a record that still stands, covering 277.25 miles (446.2 km) in a 12-hour trial race—a race to see who could ride the farthest in 12 hours. It is said that as she pedaled past the leader on her way to victory, she offered him a piece of licorice. In her later years, she often rode and competed with her daughter, Denise, who is also a cycling champion. Beryl Burton collapsed and died unexpectedly in 1996 while riding her bicycle near her home.

Susan Butcher (1954–)
Sled-dog racer

IN 1978 SUSAN BUTCHER MADE HISTORY BY BEING the first woman ever to compete in the Iditarod Trail Sled Dog Race, a grueling 1,150-mile (1,850-km) run over the frozen Alaskan landscape from Anchorage to Nome. She has since won this male-dominated race four times and is considered one of the best mushers of all time, male or female.

Butcher is the only person ever to win the Iditarod three consecutive times, from 1986 to 1988. For her victory in the 1990 Iditarod, she set a speed record, finishing in 11 days, one hour, and 53

Libby Riddles (1956–)

Susan Butcher may be the world's most successful woman musher, but she wasn't the first woman to win the Iditarod. That honor belongs to Libby Riddles, a Wisconsin native. In 1985 a blizzard struck while the race was in progress, and all the other entrants played it safe, seeking shelter from the weather. But Riddles raced on, and by the time the skies had cleared, she was five hours ahead of everyone else. Her victory made her an instant celebrity. She still races and is the author of several books for children, including *Storm Run* (1996).

minutes, which she held for four years. She has also faced her share of hardships while competing. In the 1982 Iditarod, she and her dogs were driven 10 miles off course by a blinding snowstorm and still managed to finish in second place. While racing in 1985, she and most of the dogs in her team were attacked and injured by a pregnant moose, forcing them to drop out of the race.

Although Butcher was born in Cambridge, Massachusetts, she always preferred the outdoors to city life. She moved to Alaska in the mid-1970s and later settled in the town of Eureka with her husband, the lawyer and sled racer David Monson. It is said that one of the secrets to Butcher's success is the bond she fosters with her dogs. She is able to recognize each dog's individual howl and describes her racing companions as her "best friends."

Tracy Caulkins (1963–)
Swimmer

DURING HER PRIME, TRACY CAULKINS WAS KNOWN as the most versatile female swimmer in the United States. Known for being able to win any event at any distance, she set records in every stroke. Caulkins began swimming competitively when she was a child in Winona, Minnesota, and by age 17 she was at the top of her form.

Unfortunately, in 1980 the United States boycotted the Olympics because the games' host, the Soviet Union, had violated international treaties by invading Afghanistan a few months before. Disappointed, Caulkins drove herself even harder over the next four years while at the University of Florida, and 1984 saw the high point—and the end—of her career as a swimmer. She set NCAA records in four events (the 200-meter and 400-meter individual medleys, the 200-meter butterfly, and the 100-meter breaststroke) and earned three Olympic gold medals in Los Angeles, placing first in both the 200-meter and 400-meter individual medleys. She won the third gold medal as part of the winning 400-meter relay team.

After the games, the United States Olympic Committee named her "female athlete of the year." Caulkins retired at the tender age of 21 and now coaches in Queensland, Australia. In 1990 she was inducted into the International Swimming Hall of Fame.

Florence Chadwick (1918–1995)
Swimmer

FROM A YOUNG AGE, FLORENCE CHADWICK excelled at swimming long distances in treacherous seas. The Californian started by competing in her hometown, winning the San Diego Bay Channel race when she was ten years old. Her lifelong goal, however, was to be the fastest woman to swim the English Channel. She accomplished this in 1950, with a record-breaking time of 13 hours, 20 minutes. Upon reaching English soil, Chadwick remarked, "I feel fine, I am quite prepared to swim back."

The next year she did, returning to swim in the other direction—from England to France, a much more challenging feat because of the strong tides and prevailing winds. The seas were so rough she had to take seasickness medication along the way, but Chadwick managed it in 16 hours, 22 minutes, becoming the only woman ever to swim the English Channel in both directions. Over the next several years, Chadwick set more long-distance records: in 1952 she became the first woman to swim the entire Catalina Channel, and in 1953 she swam the Straits of Gibraltar, both times besting records set by men. Chadwick eventually retired from her long-distance swimming career to become a stockbroker and swim coach. Her name was entered in the International Swimming Hall of Fame in 1970.

Conchita Cintrón (1922–)
Bullfighter

GROWING UP IN PERU, CONCHITA CINTRÓN WAS exposed early on to the "blood sport" of bullfighting. At age 12 she made her debut on horseback, the only way women were allowed in the ring at that time. Three years later, however, she was fighting as a *torera*—on foot—in Mexico. She became a successful professional bullfighter, killing approximately 1,200 bulls during her career.

Cintrón, known for her courage and beauty, became popular throughout South America. She had some success in Europe, too, but *toreras* were not yet officially sanctioned there, so she reluctantly returned to fighting on horseback. In 1949 she made her farewell appearance with a dramatic exhibition in Spain. She entered the ring on horseback and then dismounted to perform a perfect set of maneuvers before tossing her sword to the ground without killing the bull. She was arrested for fighting the bull on foot, but the crowd cheered in her favor until she was released. She then retired to Lisbon, Portugal, had six children with her nobleman husband, and became a writer.

Alice Coachman (1923–)
Track-and-field athlete, basketball player

ALICE COACHMAN COULD JUMP. A GIFTED ATHLETE, she succeeded in an era when African Americans were denied opportunities, and women were discouraged from participating in sports. By 1943, when she graduated from the Tuskegee Institute High School in Alabama, she had already attracted national attention by winning the Amateur Athletic Union (AAU) nationals in the 50-yard dash and running high jump. Over the next three years, as she worked toward a degree in dressmaking, Coachman won the running high jump, the 50-meter and 100-meter dashes, and the 400-meter relay again and again in national competition. She was also a talented basketball player and contributed to the Tuskegee team's three consecutive women's championships in the Southern Intercollegiate Athletic Conference.

World War II prevented Coachman from competing in the Olympic Games until 1948. That year in London, Coachman executed a record-breaking high jump to become the first African American woman ever to win an Olympic gold medal. After returning home to a heroine's welcome, she retired at the height of her career, married N. F. Davis, and became a teacher in her hometown of Albany, Georgia. She was inducted into the United States Track and Field Hall of Fame in 1975.

Bessie Coleman (1893–1926)
Aviator

AS A YOUNG WOMAN LIVING IN CHICAGO, BESSIE Coleman managed a chili restaurant and dreamed of flying airplanes. However, the field of aviation was still in its infancy, and the skies were dominated by white men. Not surprisingly, when this African American woman from Atlanta, Texas, applied to aviation schools in the United States, she was rejected. So she learned French and went to Europe, where she became the first African American woman to earn a pilot's license.

Returning home, Coleman became a barnstormer, or stunt flyer, the only area of aviation open to women at the time. In 1922 she made her first appearance in an American air show, attracting a lot of attention. Thousands of spectators came to Coleman's subsequent exhibitions to marvel at the female pilot. She became known as "Brave Bessie." While traveling on her barnstorming tours, she also lectured in local churches and schools about opportunities in aviation.

BLACK HERITAGE
USA
00
BESSIE COLEMAN

Coleman wanted to open her own flight school for African Americans, but that was a dream she would never fulfill.

In 1926, at the age of 33, Bessie Coleman fell to her death when the controls of her airplane jammed during a practice flight, ejecting her from her seat. In the decades since her death, Coleman's achievements have not been forgotten by the generations of people she inspired. Every Memorial Day the Tuskegee Airmen, an organization named for an all-black World War II flying squadron, fly in formation over her grave. In 1995 the United States Postal Service issued a commemorative stamp in her honor.

Georgia Coleman (1912–1940)
Diver

IDAHO NATIVE GEORGIA COLEMAN WAS SUCH A natural that, just six months after taking up diving, she went to Amsterdam to compete in the 1928 Olympics. And she did very well. She won a silver medal in the ten-meter platform event and a bronze in the three-meter springboard.

Coleman went on to dominate women's diving over the next several years. Between 1929 and 1932, she won the United States national outdoor springboard and platform titles three times. Competing indoors, she won the three-meter springboard four times. She thrilled audiences, becoming the first woman to perform a somersault dive with two and a half forward rotations successfully in competition. Once again, at the 1932 Olympics in Los Angeles, she performed impressively, winning a gold medal in the three-meter springboard and another silver in the ten-meter platform dive. Tragically, in 1937 Coleman fell victim to polio. Although at first she recovered enough to swim again, she eventually developed pneumonia as well, and died at age 28.

Nadia Comaneci (1961–)
Gymnast

IN 1967 THE GYMNASTICS COACH BELA KAROLYI caught sight of a six-year-old Nadia Comaneci playing outside a kindergarten in her hometown of Onesti, Romania. Recognizing fearlessness and a strong spirit in the young girl, he immediately began giving her lessons. At the age of eight, Comaneci started winning championship gymnastics titles and became known for her physically daring routines. But it was at the 1976 Olympics in Montreal, Canada, that Nadia's name became a household word. The world was captivated by the tiny Romanian girl who seemed to be able to perform almost-impossible moves flawlessly. She earned a perfect score of ten in seven different events—no tens had ever before been recorded in the history of Olympic gymnastics. She took home three gold medals (in the uneven parallel bars, balance beam, and all-around competition), a bronze medal for her floor exercises, and a silver team medal. At the Olympic Games in 1980 she also performed well, winning several medals and stunning her fans with her incredible feats.

At age 19, Comaneci announced her retirement, and nine years later she fled her native country for America. She ended up in Norman, Oklahoma, where she started training again and performing in exhibitions. In 1996 she married the gymnast Bart Conner. She and Conner both coach at the Bart Conner Gymnastics Academy in Norman.

Maureen Catherine Connolly (1934–1969)
Tennis player

MAUREEN CONNOLLY'S TENNIS CAREER WAS OVER by the time she was 20 years old, but her achievements were nothing less than spectacular. She started playing at age ten in her hometown of San Diego, California, and won the U.S. National junior title only three years later. She was to follow that victory with a winning streak of 56 straight matches without a loss. At age 19 "Little Mo," as the media called her, became the first woman to achieve tennis' Grand Slam—winning championship titles in Australia, France, Britain, and the United States in the same year. She won Wimbledon three times and dominated the French, Australian, and Italian national championships in 1953 and 1954. Off the court, Connolly was known as a friendly, outgoing teenager who loved music and dancing, even though she had little time for them. On the court, she dismayed her opponents with her expressionless game face and the incredible power and accuracy of her strokes.

In 1954 Connolly's right leg was crushed in a horseback-riding accident, ending her career. Soon afterward she married Norman Brinker, a former Olympic horseback rider. She continued her involvement in tennis, however, coaching and sponsoring young players through the Maureen Connolly Brinker Foundation. She was inducted into the International Tennis Hall of Fame in 1968 and died the following year of cancer at age 34.

Diane Crump (1949–)
Jockey

BORN IN CONNECTICUT, DIANE CRUMP STARTED out grooming and exercising racehorses. But by the time she was 20 years old, she was a full-fledged jockey—and a pioneer in a profession that had always been dominated by men. She became the first woman to compete in a race at a major track when she rode at Hialeah Park in Florida in 1969. She also was the first female jockey to enter a $100,000 race or to win a major feature race. And in 1970, riding a horse named Fathom, she became the first woman ever to race in the Kentucky Derby; it would be 14 years before another female jockey would appear there.

During her first 17 years as a jockey, Crump entered 1,614 races, won 235 of them, and finished second or third over 400 times. Any jockey, male or female, would be proud of such a record. Since 1986 she has worked primarily as a trainer and consultant and now manages a horse barn in Flint Hill, Virginia.

Alma Cummings (1891–unknown)
Dance marathoner

TEXAN ALMA CUMMINGS ATTRIBUTED HER SUCCESS as an endurance dancer to her vegetarian diet and the healthful climate of her home state. She danced into the record books on March 31, 1923, when she finished 27 hours of nonstop dancing with six different partners. Several dance marathon records had already been set and broken in the United States and abroad when she stepped onto the ballroom floor in New York City. And when a student at the University of Strasbourg in France broke Cummings's 27-hour record a few days later, she responded by dancing for 50 hours.

Cummings, a dance instructor who had moved to New York from San Antonio in 1922, helped to launch a craze of the 1920s when she took up marathon dancing. The fad flourished all through the Depression, despite detractors who saw it as an immoral display or who considered such physical exertion dangerous. Because women often outlasted men, dance marathons provided a new arena in which women could excel at a physical activity and played a small part in revising gender roles after World War I.

Alexandra David-Neel (1868–1969)
Explorer

ALEXANDRA DAVID WAS BORN IN FRANCE BUT found her spiritual home in Asia. As a young woman in Paris, she became an opera singer and also studied Buddhism at the Sorbonne. Touring with her opera troupe allowed her to visit Asia. In 1903 she gave up singing to become a journalist, and the next year, while in Tunisia, she married Philippe Neel, an engineer. Philippe did not travel with her, and they sometimes spent years apart, but the marriage lasted until his death in 1941.

In 1911 David-Neel became the first woman ever to interview the Dalai Lama, the spiritual leader of

Tibet, who was in exile in India. Several years of treacherous travel in pursuit of her Buddhist studies and practice brought David-Neel to the sacred city of Lhasa. She had dyed her hair and skin in order to pass as Tibetan, because foreigners were warned—upon pain of death—to keep away. The disguise and her mastery of the Tibetan language allowed her to spend two months in Lhasa. She was the first western woman ever to enter its gates.

When David-Neel arrived home in 1925, she was famous. Her government made her a chevalier of the Legion of Honor, and she was awarded gold medals by the French and Belgian geographic societies. After another eight years in China, she retired to Provence, France, where she wrote scholarly works on Tibetan culture and religion until her death a few weeks before her 101st birthday.

Anita DeFrantz (1952–)
Rower, Olympic administrator

As an African American girl growing up in Indianapolis, Indiana, Anita DeFrantz was not exposed to a wide array of sports opportunities. Consequently, she didn't discover rowing until she was a sophomore at Connecticut College. As a law student at the University of Pennsylvania, she trained hard to make the United States Olympic team. Her work paid off. In 1976 in Montreal, she won a bronze medal for rowing.

Denied the opportunity to compete when America boycotted the 1980 Olympics, DeFrantz turned her attention to a different side of sports: organizing and running the competition. In 1986 she became the first American woman to serve on the International Olympic Committee (IOC). Rising in the ranks, in 1993 she was elected to the executive board. In 1997 she became the first female vice-president of the IOC, and many of her colleagues think she will be president one day. She is also the president of the Amateur Athletic Foundation and chairs the IOC's Women and Sport Working Group. Women have made great strides as athletic competitors, but they are less well represented among sports administrators. By the example she sets and the policies she promotes, Anita DeFrantz has done much to further female leadership in athletics, both in competition and in administration.

Gail Devers (1966–)
Track-and-field athlete

As a student at the University of California at Los Angeles, sprinter and hurdler Gail Devers was told by her coach that she was destined to become an Olympic athlete. Devers was doubtful, but in 1988 the prediction came true. That was the year she set an American record for the 100-meter hurdles, which qualified her for the United States Olympic team. But during the games in Seoul, Korea, Devers performed uncharacteristically poorly and didn't make the final round.

Returning home, Devers sought medical attention for her deteriorating health. She was diagnosed with Graves' disease, a condition that affects the thyroid gland. The prescribed radiation treatment caused such a severe skin reaction on her feet that they almost had to be amputated, and the Olympic sprinter found herself unable to walk. By mid-1991, however, she had made a full recovery and staged a remarkable comeback.

The next year Devers qualified for the Olympic team again and won the 100-meter sprint in Barcelona, Spain, in a very close race. In 1993 she earned gold medals in the 100-meter sprint and the 100-meter hurdles at the World Championships in Stuttgart, Germany. For her achievements, the U.S. Olympic committee named her Athlete of the Year.

Although plagued by a hamstring injury in recent years, Devers won two gold medals at the 1996 Olympic Games in Atlanta, Georgia, and continues to compete nationally and internationally.

Lady Jane Digby el-Mesrab (1807–1881)
Adventurer

BORN INTO THE ENGLISH NOBILITY, BEAUTIFUL JANE Digby spent her adventurous life searching for true love. She married for the first time at age 17, involved herself in several affairs with European royalty, and bore seven children before finding the real love of her life.

In 1846, divorced for the third time and devastated by the accidental death of her youngest son, Jane set out for the Middle East in search of solace and escape. While exploring the deserts of Syria and its Arab cultures, she met Abdul Medjuel el-Mesrab, the younger brother of a Bedouin sheik.

Both Lady Jane's family and Medjuel's tribe were strongly opposed to their love, but the couple finally married in a traditional Muslim ceremony. They lived half of each year in a house in Damascus, Syria, where they received many European visitors. During the winter they led the traditional nomadic life of the Bedouins. Living in tents in the desert, Jane was careful to fit in—she wore the same blue gown as the

other tribeswomen, milked her husband's camels, and bathed his feet. When she was 65, she even rode into battle at his side. Their marriage lasted 26 years. In 1881 Jane died of dysentery in Medjuel's arms. She was given a Christian burial in Damascus.

Amelia Earhart (1897–1937)
Aviator

IN 1919 AMELIA EARHART RODE IN AN AIRPLANE for the first time and was changed forever by the experience. She dropped out of Columbia University's premedical program to take flying lessons and soloed for the first time in 1921. In 1928 a group sponsoring a transatlantic flight chose her as a crew member, in part because of her resemblance to Charles Lindbergh.

Earhart, who protested that she was not allowed access to anything but the log book during the 20-hour flight, instantly became famous for being the first woman to cross the Atlantic by air, and the publicity launched her career as an aviator. She lectured widely, became the aviation editor for *Cosmopolitan* magazine, and helped found the Ninety-Nines, an international organization of female aviators. She married the publicist and publisher George Putnam in 1931 but did not take his name.

In the years to come, she racked up an impressive list of aviation firsts, including becoming the first woman to fly solo across both the Atlantic and the

Pacific. On June 1, 1937, she set off to pursue another first, a 29,000-mile (46,670-km) trip around the equator. She and her navigator, Fred Noonan, were lost however, when their plane disappeared *en route* to a small island in the South Pacific. Despite an exhaustive search, the wreck of her plane was never recovered. Today, Earhart is more widely known for the mystery surrounding her death than for the considerable contributions she made to women's equality and aviation.

Krisztina Egerszegi (1974–)
Swimmer

HUNGARIAN SWIMMER KRISZTINA EGERSZEGI WAS a tiny 14 year old when she competed in the 1988 Olympic Games in Seoul, Korea—her teammates had nicknamed her "Egér," or mouse. Each of her opponents outweighed her by almost 40 pounds, but Egerszegi surprised them all by winning the 200-meter backstroke and placing second in the 100-meter backstroke. She was the youngest swimmer ever to win an Olympic gold medal.

Three years later Egerszegi took first place in the 100-meter and 200-meter backstroke races at the world championships in Australia and went on to break the standing records in both events at the European championships in Greece. At the 1992 Olympics in Spain, she earned three more gold medals, more than any female swimmer in individual events. The next year she swept the European championships in England: She won the two backstroke races, the 200-meter butterfly, and the 400-meter individual medley. After earning a gold and a bronze medal at the 1996 Olympics in Atlanta, she retired from racing, having established herself as the best backstroker of all time.

Ilona Schacherer Elek (1907–1988)
Fencer

HUNGARIAN ILONA ELEK'S LIST OF VICTORIES AS A fencer is impressive, and it would certainly have been longer if World War II hadn't dashed her hopes of competing in two Olympic competitions at the height of her career. Even so, she collected more international titles than any other woman, and she is the only woman fencer to hold two Olympic gold medals.

Ilona Elek with her father

Elek, who fenced left-handed, won the women's world foil championship in 1934 and 1935 and earned a gold medal in the individual foil competition at the 1936 Berlin Olympics. Soon war threw Europe into turmoil, and Elek did not appear at a major tournament until 1948. By then over 40 years old, she proved herself still to be in top form. She won a gold medal at the London Olympic Games and reclaimed the world foil championship title in 1951. The next year at the Helsinki Olympics, she very nearly repeated her gold-medal performance. After winning the first 20 matches, she faltered in the last three and, by a slim margin, was awarded the silver.

Janet Evans (1971–)
Swimmer

JANET EVANS LEARNED TO SWIM ABOUT THE SAME time she learned to walk. She trained and competed all through her school years in suburban Los Angeles, and she always managed to earn high grades.

In 1987 Evans's work paid off when she competed in the United States long-course championship and broke two world records, in the 800- and 1,500-meter freestyle events. Later that year she toppled the 400-meter freestyle record at the U.S. Open. Although she had to bring homework with her to Seoul, Korea, tiny Evans (who at the time stood at just over five feet tall) dominated the 1988 summer Olympic Games, winning three gold medals. She also won the hearts of fans with her vivacious personality and was swamped with media attention. She went on to win another Olympic gold medal in 1992 and was her team's captain in the 1996 summer games. She graduated from the University of Southern California in 1994 with a degree in communications and continues to promote her sport. One of the fastest swimmers ever to take to the water, many of her records remain unbroken.

Christine Marie Evert (1954–)
Tennis player

AT THE TENDER AGE OF 16, CHRIS EVERT WAS attracting national attention on the tennis court, but as a player she was anything but "tender." Evert faced every opponent with unwavering skill, a steely game face, and a wicked two-handed backhand stroke.

"Chrissie's" father, tennis teacher Jimmy Evert, noticed her talent early on and began coaching her. In 1971 she competed in her first U.S. Open, losing in the semifinals to one of the world's best players, Billie Jean King. The following year she graduated from high school in Fort Lauderdale, Florida, and turned pro on her 18th birthday. By 1974 Evert was the top-ranked woman player in the world, and in 1976 she became the first woman to earn a million dollars in prize money. Her astonishing record includes winning three singles titles at Wimbledon, seven singles titles in the French Open, and six singles titles in the U.S. Open. Her 15-year rivalry with tennis great Martina Navratilova thrilled the press and helped make women's tennis a popular sports attraction.

Evert also served as president of the Women's International Tennis Association for nine terms. She retired from her professional career in 1989 and was inducted into the International Tennis Hall of Fame in 1995. She and her second husband, skier Andy Mill, have three sons and live in Colorado.

Amy Feng (1969–)
Table tennis player

WHILE ENROLLED IN AN ELITE SPORTS SCHOOL IN Tianjin, China, as a teenager, table tennis player Amy Feng almost lost her desire to play because of the unforgiving schedule. She was forced to train over six hours a day, leaving her little time for anything else. All that work paid off, however. By 1986 she had placed second in the Chinese national championships and was ranked 26th in the world.

In 1991 Feng met American Andrew Tan, an amateur player who was on vacation in China to train. She emigrated to the United States the following year and married him. Although she was happy to be released from the rigors of Chinese training, Feng's game suffered. In China, a Communist country, athletes' training was subsidized by the state, but in America, Feng had to support herself and pay for her own training, a difficult task. She still ranked as America's top female player, however, winning the U.S. table tennis championship in 1995. She continues to train and compete, supporting her career by coaching others.

Peggy Gale Fleming (1948–)
Figure skater

PEGGY FLEMING WAS A GIFTED DANCER, AND IT showed in her skating. She was one of the most technically skilled yet artistically graceful skaters the sport has ever seen. Fleming, a Californian, learned to skate when her family spent two years in Cleveland, Ohio, where the chilly winters made the sport popular. In 1961 Fleming's coach, Billy Kipp, and the entire U.S. team were killed in a plane crash on the way to a competition. If she hadn't been too young, Fleming might have been with them. At age 15 she became the youngest woman to win a senior national championship,

the first of her five consecutive U.S. national titles. In Davos, Switzerland, in 1966, Fleming became the first American woman in almost a decade to win the world figure skating championship, and she retained that title for the next two years.

While studying dance and biology at Colorado College, Fleming trained for the 1968 Olympics, to be held in Grenoble, France. She was the only American to win a gold medal that year. Shortly thereafter, she retired from amateur competition. As a professional skater, she has appeared in television specials and toured with shows such as the Ice Follies. Fleming has served as a goodwill ambassador for UNICEF and sat on the President's Council on Physical Fitness. Since her own experience with breast cancer in 1998, she has worked to promote awareness of the disease and to raise funds for research.

Clare Francis (1946–)
Sailor

As a child, Clare Francis developed a passion for sailing while training to become a dancer at the Royal Ballet School in London. She gave up dancing for a career in economics and a few years later purchased her first boat, the *Gulliver G*. In 1973, on a dare, Francis sailed across the Atlantic alone. Those 37 days were grueling, wet, and lonely. Returning home, she announced she would never do such a thing again.

But the thrill of racing soon outweighed her memories of the discomfort involved. Francis entered the

> "I had now to decide whether the loneliness, the sheer discomfort and the likelihood of being frightened a great deal of the time were going to be worth that nice feeling of achievement I hoped to enjoy after the finish. . . . [T]his was going to be my last big race before carrying out my firm intention of running to fat in a rose-covered cottage. And how could I say 'Never again' with any conviction if I hadn't had a really horrible time?"
>
> **CLARE FRANCIS**
> **on deciding to enter the Transatlantic race**
> *Come Hell or High Water*

Observer Royal Western Single-Handed Transatlantic Race in 1976. She crossed the finish line in 29 days, taking 13th place overall and breaking the women's transatlantic record by three days. The following year she skippered a boat with a crew of 11 in the Whitbread Round the World Race, which took seven months to finish. Again, she vowed to stop racing, and this time she kept her promise, retiring from competition to become a writer. In addition to novels, she has published two autobiographical books, *Come Hell or High Water* (1977) and *Come Wind or Weather* (1978).

Dawn Fraser (1937–)
Swimmer

As the youngest of eight children, Dawn Fraser was not encouraged to swim but still found her way to the pool near her home in Sydney, Australia. She raced for the first time at the ripe old age of 16 and was already 19 when she joined the Australian women's team at the 1956 Olympics in Melbourne, Australia. Fraser easily took the gold in the 100-meter freestyle and returned to Olympic competition in Rome four years later to win that event again, setting a world record by completing it in under a minute.

At the 1964 Summer Olympic Games in Tokyo, Japan, Fraser was 27 years old—practically a senior citizen by swimming standards. She had also suffered a broken neck in a car accident seven months earlier. Even so, she kept herself in top shape and won her third consecutive Olympic gold medal that summer in the 100-meter freestyle. Fraser retired after the Tokyo games, but she has remained popular with her fellow Australians. From 1988 to 1991 she served in the parliament of New South Wales.

Fu Mingxia (1979–)
Diver

A native of Hubei Province in China, Fu Mingxia was recruited by her government for athletic training when she was seven. She didn't even know how to swim before she started learning to dive. Soon she was winning international titles, such as the platform diving event at the Goodwill

Games in 1990, and the world championship the following year. At the Barcelona Olympics in 1992 she easily won the gold medal, and the world marveled at the way the slender girl disappeared into the water without even making a splash. She competed in the platform and the springboard competitions at the 1996 Olympic Games, winning both and becoming only the second female diver to earn gold medals in two consecutive Olympics.

Fu's status as an athlete allows her special privileges at home, such as better housing and a higher than average income. In 1996 she enrolled at Tsinghua University in Peking, putting an end to the intense training sessions of her childhood—up to ten hours daily. However, she has not yet ruled out the possibility that she will compete in the 2000 Olympics in Sydney, Australia.

Althea Gibson (1927–)
Tennis player

As an African American athlete, Althea Gibson overcame many obstacles to succeed in the privileged world of competitive tennis. Raised in Harlem in New York City with few advantages and little encouragement, the teenage Gibson frequently skipped school to go to movies or play sports like stickball and paddle tennis on the street. Her athleticism did not go unnoticed. The boxer Sugar Ray Robinson became her friend and adviser, and eventually two wealthy black doctors sponsored her training. Initially barred from many competitions because of race, Gibson drew a lot of attention while playing with the predominantly black American Tennis Association, where she won several championships. In 1950 Gibson became the first black person, man or woman, invited to play in a United States Lawn Tennis Association event, the U.S. Open tournament at Forest Hills, New York.

Suddenly other tournaments opened their doors, too. It took Gibson a few years to hit her stride, but then she began an impressive winning streak. In 1956 she claimed another first for African American tennis players—male or female—by winning a grand slam event, the French Open. In both 1957 and 1958, she won the singles and doubles titles at Wimbledon as well as the U.S. Open championship.

After retiring from tournament tennis at the age of 32, Gibson performed with the Harlem Globetrotters basketball team, became a professional golfer, and served as New Jersey state athletic commissioner. She was inducted into the International Tennis Hall of Fame in 1971 and the International Women's Sports Hall of Fame in 1980.

Isabel Godin des Odonais (1728–1792)
Traveler

ISABEL DE GRANDMAISON Y BRUNO WAS BORN INTO a prominent family in Riobamba, in what is now Ecuador. At age 13, she married Jean Godin des Odonais, an assistant for a French scientific expedition in the Andes. Jean stayed with his pregnant wife when the expedition moved on, promising to catch up with them. However, during the next six years Isabel gave birth to four children, and she was not able to travel. Finally in 1749 Jean set off alone, promising to come back to Riobamba as soon as he could. Twenty-one years passed before Isabel and Jean saw each other again.

Jean ended up in French Guiana, where he waited 15 years for the Portuguese colonial government to grant him access to the Amazon. Meanwhile, their children all died of fever. Finally, in 1769, Isabel set out to meet her husband, accompanied by a party that included two of her brothers, a nephew, 31 Native Americans, and three Frenchmen. Within five weeks, everyone but Isabel had either deserted the group or died. She wandered, lost and alone, for over a week, before finding help.

Her subsequent journey down the entire length of the Amazon is the first documented expedition of that route by a woman. Isabel arrived in Cayenne in 1770. Despite all that had happened, they were overjoyed to be reunited. The couple sailed to France in 1773 and settled at Jean's family estate in Saint-Amand-Montrond. There Isabel's story of loyalty and endurance made her a local heroine.

Diana Golden (1963–)
Skier

GROWING UP IN THE SUBURBS OF BOSTON, DIANA Golden always considered herself a "klutz." She hated all sports, except skiing. At age 12 she discovered she had bone cancer and had to have her right leg amputated, but she was back on her feet within a few weeks. She learned to walk with a prosthetic leg; when it came to skiing, though, she found she could maneuver very well using just one ski. Golden joined her high school ski team and then the United States Disabled Ski Team. By the

end of her senior year, she had placed first in the downhill and second in the giant slalom races at the World Handicapped Championships.

Golden quit skiing while she attended Dartmouth College, but a trip with friends in 1984 rekindled her enthusiasm. Resuming her training, she became the first disabled ski racer to be sponsored by a major ski equipment company, Rossignol. She also campaigned to allow disabled skiers to compete on equal footing with regularly abled skiers. As a result, in 1985, the United States Ski Association created the "Golden Rule," which established a more equitable method of seeding competitors.

Golden went on to win and place in races against both disabled and regularly abled skiers. She received many awards, including the 1991 Flo Hyman award for outstanding achievements in and commitment to her sport. That same year she retired from racing. She continues to work on behalf of disabled athletes.

Evonne Fay Goolagong (1951–)
Tennis player

EVONNE GOOLAGONG, ONE OF AUSTRALIA'S FINEST athletes, was the first aboriginal Australian to achieve international athletic success. Evonne's father worked as a sheep shearer in their hometown of Barellan, and because they had eight children to feed, her parents had a hard time making ends meet. At age five, Evonne began earning pocket money by retrieving tennis balls at the local tennis club. By the time she was ten, however, she was training to be a tennis player herself and living with the family of one of Australia's top coaches, Vic Edwards.

Goolagong became a professional tennis player in 1971 and won both the French Open and Wimbledon that year. She continued to reach the finals in international championships throughout the decade. For four consecutive years, between 1974 and 1977, she won the singles and doubles titles in the Australian Open, and she helped her team to win three Federation Cups. In 1980 she surprised everyone by defeating Tracy Austin and then Chris Evert in singles competition at Wimbledon. By that time she had had her first child with her husband, Roger Cawley—she was the first mother to win a Wimbledon singles title in 66 years. Goolagong retired from tennis in 1983 and was inducted into the International Tennis Hall of Fame five years later.

Stephanie (Steffi) Graf (1969–)
Tennis player

AT AGE THREE, STEFFI GRAF WAS PLAYING TENNIS on an improvised court in the basement of her home in Bruhl, Germany. Ten years later she quit school to join the women's professional tour. She was ranked 124th in the world at the time, the second-youngest player ever to be given a ranking. In 1987 she won 70 of 72 matches and 11 of the 13 tournaments she entered.

However, it was in 1988 that Graf, by then ranked number one, really demonstrated her superiority. She achieved tennis' Grand Slam—winning the Australian Open, the French Open, Wimbledon, and the U.S. Open all in the same year. During that summer, between Grand-Slam victories, she traveled to Seoul, Korea, to capture an Olympic gold medal, too.

In the 1990s Graf was challenged by newcomer Monica Seles, who even sometimes claimed the number one ranking. Their ongoing rivalry excited

tennis fans worldwide and sharpened the player's competitive edge. When Seles was stabbed in the back by an irrational Graf fan in 1993 and had to stop competing for two years, Steffi was mortified and saddened. Graf is no longer the top-ranked player, but she held that status for an impressive total of 374 weeks overall. With her incredible speed and famous forehand, she remains a tough competitor on the professional circuit and is sure to go down in history as one of tennis' greatest players.

Michele Granger (1970–)
Softball pitcher

MICHELE GRANGER, A LEFT-HANDER FROM Anchorage, Alaska, learned to pitch from her father, Mike, who employed some unorthodox, but effective, coaching methods, such as tying Michele to a tree to correct a bad habit in her footing. She was a world-class pitcher by the time she was in high school and was named Sportswoman of the Year in 1986 by the United States Olympic Committee. The teenager pitched a no-hitter in the 1987 world championships and went on to help the U.S. team win several gold medals in the Pan American games over the next few years.

While she was a student at the University of California at Berkeley, Granger broke the NCAA record for strikeouts. In the 1995 Pan Am competition, she pitched four shutouts and one perfect game. Michele's fastball has been clocked at over 70 miles per hour (113 kph). Because the dimensions of the playing fields are different, this is equivalent to a 96-mile-per-hour (154-kph) pitch in baseball. As the starting pitcher for Team USA in the 1996 Olympics in Atlanta, Georgia, Granger helped to defeat China 3–1 to win the gold. It was the first time women's softball was ever played as a medal sport in the Olympics.

Beatrice Grimshaw (1871–1953)
Traveler, writer

BY THE TIME SHE WAS 30 YEARS OLD, BEATRICE Grimshaw was a well-known journalist in Dublin and had set a bicycling record for distance covered during a 24-hour ride. But Grimshaw longed to travel. So she left her Irish homeland and moved to London, where, in 1906, she made a gutsy deal with shipping companies: She would provide them with ample press coverage in return for free passage to the South Pacific.

The scheme was so successful that Grimshaw was able to spend the next three decades traveling. She visited French Polynesia, Fiji, the Solomon Islands, New Guinea, New Caledonia, Borneo, and Java, among other places—many of them known for their mosquitoes, fevers, and cannibals, as well as their natural beauty. During her time abroad, she made Papua New Guinea her home base and lived there in houses she built herself. She ran a plantation, prospected for diamonds, went diving in the Torres Strait, and became the first white woman to navigate the Sepik and Fly rivers of New Guinea. Among Grimshaw's more than 40 books are the travel narrative *From Fiji to the Cannibal Islands* (1907) and a novel entitled *The Red Gods Call* (1910), which, like all of her fiction, was set in the South Seas. After 1939 she retired to a more sedate life in New South Wales, Australia.

Janet Guthrie (1938–)
Auto racer

JANET GUTHRIE WAS NEVER AFRAID TO CHALLENGE herself. The Iowa native had a pilot's license by the time she was 17. After graduating from the University of Michigan with a physics degree in 1960, she became one of four women to qualify for the National Aeronautics and Space Administration's scientist-astronaut program. However, NASA required a Ph.D. for full participation, so she was subsequently disqualified. Around that time, she started racing cars, and in 1967 she quit her job as an aerospace engineer to race full-time.

When, at first, no one was willing to hire a woman driver, Guthrie outfitted her own race car. She became the first woman to participate in the Winston Cup series—sponsored by the National Association for Stock Car Auto Racing, or NASCAR—when she entered the Charlotte World 600 in 1976. Racing for the entire 600 miles (965 km) without a relief driver, she finished in 15th place. The following year, mechanical troubles forced her out of the Indianapolis 500 after 27 laps. Then in 1978, she triumphantly reached

the finish line in Indianapolis in ninth place, the first woman ever to complete that esteemed event. The driver's suit and helmet she wore that day are on display at the Smithsonian Institute in Washington, D.C.

Mia Hamm (1972–)
Soccer player

THE DAUGHTER OF A MILITARY COLONEL, MIA Hamm lived in Alabama, California, Texas, and Italy while she was growing up. She learned to love sports from her older brother, Garrett, who encouraged her and chose her for his team when the kids at the military base played soccer games.

By the time she was a teenager, Hamm's exceptional talent for soccer was apparent. At age 15 she became the youngest person ever to play for the United States National team. While studying political science at the University of North Carolina from 1989 to 1993, she played for her college and the national team. She helped the UNC Tar Heels win the NCAA championships four times, and in 1991 the national team won the first-ever Women's World Cup, held in China. In 1995 she demonstrated her versatility, playing forward, midfield, and goalkeeper during the second Women's World Cup in Sweden. She led the U.S. team to a gold medal in the 1996

Olympics and helped them to win the 1999 Women's World Cup. Hamm continues to be at the peak of her skills and draws thousands of devoted fans wherever she plays. Although she is intensely shy, she takes her role as ambassador for women's soccer seriously and works hard to promote her beloved sport.

Judith Devlin Hashman (1935–)
Badminton player

JUDY DEVLIN, A NATIVE OF WINNIPEG, CANADA, learned badminton from her father, Frank, who won the English singles championship six times. Badminton is a fast and ferocious game. The shuttlecock whizzes by at speeds of up to 150 miles per hour (242 kph), and a typical match keeps players in action for twice as long as a tennis match. Consequently, they must be astonishingly good athletes—and Judy was. In addition to badminton, she played on the United States lacrosse team for five years, achieved a national ranking in tennis, and was an accomplished field hockey, basketball, and squash player.

Devlin started winning junior championships when she was 13. In 1954 she won the junior, senior, and world singles titles, as well as the All-England and United States doubles titles, in which she played with her sister, Susan. In the early 1960s, she married a fellow champion badminton player, Dick Hashman, but she didn't let that slow her career. By 1967 Judy had won over 50 national women's singles and doubles championships all over the world. She was inducted

> "When my opponent becomes merely a blank face and the relationship is between me and the shuttle, then I get this miraculous feeling of friendliness, understanding, and affection almost for the small white object that does my bidding so well. It is always preceded by a small chill which runs the length of my spine and instils within me a calmness and confidence of which I would ordinarily be incapable—and it instils this in spite of my cold hands and clammy feet!"
>
> JUDY DEVLIN HASHMAN
> *Badminton a Champion's Way*, 1969

into the Helms National Badminton Hall of Fame in 1963 and the International Women's Sports Hall of Fame in 1995. Today she lives in England and works as a coach.

Sonja Henie (1912–1969)
Figure skater, film actor

BORN INTO A WEALTHY OSLO, NORWAY, FAMILY, Sonja Henie was a natural on the ice from the time she was five. Taking advantage of her ballet lessons to improve her routines, she won the Norwegian figure skating championship in 1923. As she trained and competed over the next several years,

she consistently used balletic choreography to achieve a more graceful, entertaining performance than the series of disconnected, technical moves her competitors executed. She also wore a shorter skirt than the others, to allow for freer movement. Her unique style won her ten world championships in as many years, three Olympic gold medals, and perhaps most importantly, transformed the sport into a popular event, inspiring thousands of girls to give it a try.

Henie retired from competition in 1936 and set out for Hollywood to become a movie star. She signed a five-year contract with Twentieth Century–Fox and made a series of enormously popular skating films.

Only Clark Gable and Shirley Temple could have claimed to have more fans. During the 1960s Henie and her third husband, Norwegian ship owner Niels Onstad, began investing the fortune she had amassed from her ice shows and movies—over $47 million—in works of art. They opened the Sonja Henie-Niels Onstad Art Center outside of Oslo in 1968. Henie died of leukemia the following year.

Lynn Hill (1961–)
Rock climber

Lᴄʏɴɴ Hɪʟʟ ɴᴇᴠᴇʀ ʙᴇʟɪᴇᴠᴇᴅ ɪɴ ʜᴏʟᴅɪɴɢ ᴍᴇɴ ᴀɴᴅ women to different standards of achievement, and she worked hard to equalize the sport of rock climbing. This native Californian not only achieved the status of best female rock climber, she became one of the *top five* climbers in the world.

Hill began climbing at age 14, and five years later she became the first woman to climb one of the most difficult rock faces in the world, Ophir Broke, in Telluride, Colorado. After that she focused on climbing as a full-time career, paying her living expenses with odd jobs. She even appeared on a television program called "*Survival of the Fittest,*" in which contestants ran obstacle courses. During the 1989 World Cup competition in Lyon, France, on an adjustable, human-made cliff, Hill defeated all but two climbers, both men, dramatically demonstrating that women could indeed compete as equals in the sport. The following year in Cimaï, France, she became the first woman to complete a climb with an extremely difficult rating, 5.14.

Hill has retired from competition but travels internationally to promote her sport. She has continued her daring feats. In 1998 she became the first woman to free climb "Midnight Lightning," a boulder in Yosemite, California.

Flora (Flo) Hyman (1954–1986)
Volleyball player

Fʟᴏ Hʏᴍᴀɴ ʜᴇʟᴘᴇᴅ ᴛᴏ ʙʀɪɴɢ ᴡᴏᴍᴇɴ'ꜱ ᴠᴏʟʟᴇʏʙᴀʟʟ into the spotlight. At six feet, five inches (2 m) tall, this African American woman from California used her stature to supreme advantage. Her impressive performances on her high school team won

her a scholarship to the University of Houston in 1974. At first she played on both her college and the U.S. national teams. In 1976, although she was named outstanding collegiate player, she decided to train exclusively with the U.S. team. The team's performance record had been disappointing, and Hyman's charismatic presence immediately made a difference. The judges and coaches at the 1981 World Cup in Tokyo voted her the world's best spiker, or power hitter. They also chose her for the multinational All-World Cup team; she was the first American woman to receive that honor. Three years later she led a revitalized U.S. team to a silver medal at the Olympics in Los Angeles.

In 1986 the 31-year-old Hyman was playing as a professional in Japan when she suddenly collapsed and died. It was discovered that she had suffered a ruptured aorta, the result of a genetic heart disorder called Marfan's Syndrome, which also causes its victims to grow unusually tall. In 1987 the Women's Sports Foundation established the Flo Hyman Award in her memory, to honor female athletes who embody the "dignity, spirit, and commitment to excellence" that Hyman displayed during her career.

Dame Naomi James (1949–)
Sailor, historian

Nᴀᴏᴍɪ Pᴏᴡᴇʀ ᴡᴀꜱ ᴀ ꜱʜʏ ᴄʜɪʟᴅ, ʙᴜᴛ ꜱʜᴇ dreamed of heroic feats. At age 22, determined to see the world, she left the dairy farm in Hawkes Bay, New Zealand, where she had grown up.

To support her traveling life, she worked as a hairdresser and, later, taught English in Austria. When she met her future husband, the sailor Rob James, during a trip to England in 1975, he introduced her to his sport. Within two years of her initial voyage—which was marred by seasickness—Naomi set out to become the first woman to sail around the world alone.

She had never handled a boat by herself before, and she had several close calls, including almost drowning when she capsized near Cape Horn. Nevertheless she pulled the feat off in record time. To honor her accomplishment, Queen Elizabeth named her a Dame Commander of the British Empire. James went on to become the only woman to finish the *Observer* Transatlantic Race in 1980, setting a women's record for a solo transatlantic crossing. In 1982 Naomi and Rob won the Double-Handed Round Britain Race together. After Rob was killed in an accident the following year, Naomi retired from competitive sailing. She has since written several books about her own adventures and maritime history.

Amy Johnson (1903–1941)
Aviator

AMY JOHNSON WAS WORKING AS A SECRETARY IN London in 1928, when she became fascinated by the planes passing over her apartment on their way to an airfield nearby. Two years later she had not only obtained her pilot's license and ground engineer's certificate, she made history by flying solo from England to Australia. Although she was relatively inexperienced, she managed the 13,000-mile (20,920-km) trip in just under 20 days.

Johnson hadn't set any records that time, but she became an instant, international celebrity. She was dubbed the "Queen of the Air" and "the Empire's Great Little Woman" by the press, who followed her everywhere. In 1931 she flew from England to Tokyo, and five years later she broke the standing record for flying from London to Cape Town and back. Johnson found coping with the stress of her fame difficult; her marriage to fellow pilot James Mollison failed as a result. When World War II broke out in 1939, Johnson volunteered for Great Britain's Air Transport Auxiliary Force. In January 1941, while delivering a plane to a site near

Early Flying Conditions

In the early days, airplane travel was nothing like riding in a modern passenger jet. Cold weather penetrated the small planes, chilling the pilots and sometimes freezing the meters. The noise of the engine was so loud that pilots had to shout to communicate. During her solo flight to Australia, Amy Johnson pumped gas by hand from a storage tank to the fuel tank, and the fumes made her sick. It was also important not to overload the plane. Toward the end of their final flight, Amelia Earhart and her copilot unloaded anything that added weight, including parachutes.

Oxford, she got lost flying in dense fog and ran out of fuel. She crashed into the Thames River and drowned in the icy water before rescuers could reach her.

Lynn Jonckowski (1954–)
Bull rider

LYNN "JONNIE" JONCKOWSKI ALWAYS HAD A strong competitive drive, but even though she grew up in the West—in Billings, Montana—she didn't start out to become a rodeo champion. She wanted to be an Olympic pentathlete, until a back injury in 1975 ruined her chances.

In 1976 Jonckowski entered the bull-riding contest at an all-women's rodeo on a whim and was hooked on the extremely dangerous sport, which involves trying to stay on the back of a 1,500-pound (680-kg) bull, who's trying equally hard to rid himself of his unwanted passenger. She was seriously injured several times but never discouraged. In the 1986 world championship competition, the nerves behind Jonckowski's knee were severed when the bull stepped on her after a fall. Ignoring her doctor's fear that a blood clot might cause a heart attack or stroke, Jonckowski had herself lifted off her crutches and onto the back of a bull the next day—and that ride won her the title. She won again in 1988, and in 1991 she was inducted into the Cowgirl Hall of Fame in Hereford, Texas.

Lena Jordan (1879?–?)
Trapeze artist

L ENA, BORN IN POVERTY IN RUSSIA, LEFT HER HOME in Riga at a young age, when her parents apprenticed her to an American family of aerialists who were passing through town. She was chosen because she was small and light, but by the time she was 18, she was also extraordinarily strong. Although she weighed only 95 pounds, Lena's upper-body strength allowed her to perform incredible gymnastic trapeze stunts with her adopted family, the Flying Jordans.

In 1897 the Flying Jordans toured Australia, where the press reported that Lena regularly performed a triple back somersault in midair as she flew between two catchers. The triple somersault—called *salto mortale*, or "somersault of death," by the Spanish—had never been accomplished before. Over time, though, Lena's achievement was forgotten, and in 1909 credit for the feat was given to a man, Ernest Clarke. By then Lena appears to have left the act; nothing else is known about her. It wasn't until 1975 that the *Guinness Book of World Records* checked the historical documentation and properly recognized Lena Jordan as the first person ever to perform a triple somersault.

Karen and Sarah Josephson (1964–)
Synchronized swimmers

K AREN AND SARAH JOSEPHSON WERE BORN identical twins in Bristol, Connecticut. They learned to swim at age five and started training together three years later, taking advantage of their close relationship to help them coordinate their movements

flawlessly in the water. They worked out with weights, swam long distances, and took yoga and dance lessons. At age 16 they joined the United States national team and the next year enrolled at Ohio State University, where they were members of the undefeated Ohio State team and graduated with honors in 1985.

The twins dreamed of competing together in the Olympics. In 1984 only Sarah made the team, as an alternate. But in 1988 they went to the games in Seoul, Korea, where they won a silver medal in the duet event. That was the last time they were second-best. Their overall duet score at the 1991 world championships was the highest in synchronized swimming history. And in 1992 they won the gold at the Barcelona Olympics, receiving several perfect marks for technical merit and artistic impression. That medal represented their 16th consecutive victory, another synchronized swimming record. The Josephsons retired shortly afterward, having established themselves at the top of their sport. They are one of only two duet pairs in the International Swimming Hall of Fame.

Joan Joyce (1940–)
Softball player, golfer

J OAN JOYCE WAS A SUPERB ALL-AROUND ATHLETE. She excelled at everything she attempted— basketball, volleyball, bowling, golf—but her *tour de force* was softball. Her slingshot style of pitching resulted in a fastball clocked at 116 miles per hour (187 kph). During her 22-year amateur career, Joyce's team won 509 games and lost only 33. She pitched 105 no-hitters and 33 perfect games. She also sometimes played first base and had a career hitting average of .327. Mostly she played for the Raybestos Brakettes of Stratford, Connecticut (not far from her hometown of Waterbury). She joined the team when she was 13 and eventually led them to 11 national championships. During her four years at Chapman College in California, Joyce played for the Orange Lionettes.

After resigning her amateur status in 1975, Joyce worked hard to establish women's softball as a professional sport in the United States. She cofounded the International Women's Professional Softball Association (IWPSA) and became the star player, part-owner, and manager of the Connecticut Falcons. Her team won the World Series Championship for the next four years. In 1979 IWPSA folded for lack of money, but by then Joyce had embarked on a second career. She became a professional golfer. She was voted into the National Softball Hall of Fame in 1983.

Jackie Joyner-Kersee (1962–)
Track-and-field athlete

GROWING UP IN POVERTY IN EAST ST. LOUIS, Illinois, Jackie Joyner played basketball and volleyball and earned high grades in school. She was captivated by the televised track-and-field competition of the 1976 Olympics and started training. By the age of 14, she had won her first of four consecutive national junior pentathlon championships.

Jackie accepted a basketball scholarship to the University of California, Los Angeles, where she met her future husband and coach, Bob Kersee. He persuaded her to concentrate on track and field and helped her train for the heptathlon, a series of seven events requiring a myriad of skills, including running, jumping, and throwing. Winners are determined by the number of points they receive overall.

Jackie dominated her sport and always performed well at the Olympics. At the 1984 Olympic Games, she suffered from a pulled hamstring, but she still placed second in the heptathlon. In 1988 she was the shining star of the Olympics when she won a gold medal in the heptathlon *and* in an individual event, the long jump. She won the heptathlon gold again in 1992 and earned a bronze medal in the long jump. Her final Olympic appearance before her retirement was in 1996 in Atlanta. There she won a bronze medal in the long jump but had to withdraw from the heptathlon because of another hamstring injury. She is considered by many to be one of the greatest athletes of all time.

Dorothy Kamenshek (1925–)
Baseball player

DOTTIE KAMENSHEK GREW UP PLAYING SOFTBALL in her home state of Ohio and was recruited to play for the All-American Girls Professional Baseball League for their first season in 1943. Kamenshek played for the Rockford, Illinois, Peaches for almost a decade, initially as an outfielder and later at first base. A talented ball player with a strength for batting, her career batting average was an impressive .292 (this means that 29.2 percent of her hits allowed her to get safely to first base or farther). In the nearly 3,800 times she came to bat, she struck out only 81 times. In 1950 a men's professional baseball league attempted to recruit her, but she turned them down because she thought it was a publicity stunt.

Kamenshek was chosen for the women's All-Star team seven times during her professional career. By 1953, however, increasingly painful back injuries forced her into retirement. She went to college and in 1958 received a degree in physical therapy from Marquette University in Wisconsin. Later she moved to California, where she became head of the Los Angeles Crippled Children's Services Department.

Annette Kellerman (1888–1975)
Swimmer

AUSTRALIAN SWIMMER ANNETTE KELLERMAN took up the sport as a girl to rehabilitate her bowed legs, sparking a lifelong passion that would permanently change water sports for women. Kellerman excelled at racing, distance swimming, diving, and water acrobatics. She performed in diving exhibitions in Sydney and Melbourne, toured the world with aquatic shows, and swam in Hollywood movies.

When long-distance swimming became popular, Kellerman toured Europe, swimming rivers such as the Seine and the Danube. She tried twice, unsuccessfully, to swim the English Channel. Her fame reached its peak in 1907, when she swam across Boston Harbor wearing a swimsuit that scandalized the world. In a dramatic departure from the standard women's bathing costume, with its modest long skirts and sleeves, Kellerman had designed a skintight, one-piece, V-neck affair, with cap sleeves and Bermuda-length legs. She was arrested in Boston for indecent exposure, but she continued to wear her suit, garnering praise for her figure and starting a trend in swimwear that allowed women to accomplish greater feats in the water. Throughout her life she advocated women's rights and physical fitness. She is memorialized in the International Swimming Hall of Fame and is the subject of the 1952 biographical film, *Million Dollar Mermaid*, starring her American counterpart, Esther Williams.

Billie Jean King (1943–)
Tennis player

California native Billie Jean Moffitt gave up softball for tennis at age 11, because it was a more socially acceptable sport for girls. By age 17 she was competing at Wimbledon, and she had won three doubles titles there when she married the lawyer and sports promoter Larry King in 1965. In the course of her career, she won a record 20 Wimbledon titles and numerous other championships in both singles and doubles competition. She was an incredible force in women's tennis, not only as one of the world's greatest players but as an outspoken advocate for the rights of female players.

In 1973 Billie Jean King was challenged by former tennis professional Bobby Riggs, who boasted that any man, no matter how old—he was 55—could beat any woman, no matter how powerful. It was a highly publicized "Battle of the Sexes." A live audience of 30,000 gathered at the Houston Astrodome, and another 60 million people watched on television as King demolished Riggs in three straight sets (and earned an unprecedented $100,000).

King went on to found the Women's Tennis Association, a labor union for female players and organized the first women-only tennis tour, with prize amounts equal to those men earned. With her husband, she cofounded *WomenSports* magazine in 1974 and, two years later, created the organization World TeamTennis. King is still affiliated with WTT, now active in hundreds of American cities, which sponsors annual coed team championships for both professional and amateur players.

Mary Henrietta Kingsley (1862–1900)
Traveler, naturalist

Londoner Mary Kingsley was not raised for a life of adventure. Instead she was expected to take care of her invalid mother and perform domestic duties while her father, a physician who fancied himself an explorer, was away on expeditions. Lonely and isolated, she was not given a formal education, but she had free access to her father's scientific library, which she devoured. When both her parents died in the same year, Mary suddenly found herself free to travel. In her remarkable journeys, she wandered far from her stifling roots and found expression for her vast intelligence, humane spirit, and unfailing courage. She also cultivated an image as the eccentric English lady who tromped cheerily through the world's wildest jungles (and survived many appalling misadventures). Her two books, *Travels in West Africa* (1897) and *West African Studies* (1899), were enormously popular.

> "Now a crocodile drifting down in deep water, or lying asleep with its jaws open on a sand-bank in the sun, is a picturesque adornment to the landscape when you are on the deck of a steamer, and you can write home about it and frighten your relations on your behalf; but when you are away among the swamps in a small dug-out canoe, and that crocodile and his relations are awake—a thing he makes a point of being at flood tide because of fish coming along. . . you get frightened on your own behalf. For crocodiles can, and often do, in such places, grab at people in small canoes."
>
> MARY KINGSLEY
> *Travels in West Africa*, 1897

Kingsley made her two expeditions in the early 1890s, visiting Cameroon, Gabon, and the Congo. Traveling as a trader, she became the first westerner to meet the Fang cannibal tribes. While there she collected specimens of previously undiscovered fish and reptile species, which she presented to the British Museum. She strongly disapproved of the white missionaries' efforts to westernize Africans and became an outspoken champion of African tribal culture in her lectures and writings, much to the dismay of the British Colonial Office.

Kingsley intended to return to her beloved West Africa. However, while serving as a volunteer nurse during the Boer Wars in South Africa, she contracted typhoid fever and died. She was buried at sea, according to her last wishes.

Irena Kirszenstein-Szewinska (1946–)
Sprinter, long jumper

BORN TO JEWISH PARENTS IN RUSSIA AND RAISED in Poland, Irena Kirszenstein-Szewinska was an unknown teenager when she competed internationally at the 1964 Olympics in Tokyo. She burst into the headlines that year, claiming silver medals in the 200-meter race and the long jump and helping to win the team gold in the 400-meter relay. By the time she won four medals in the 1966 European Championships, Kirszenstein was a heroine at home. She couldn't walk down the streets of Warsaw without being recognized.

During the 1968 Olympics in Mexico City, Irena set a world record in the 200-meter and won a bronze medal in the 100-meter event. She earned another bronze in the 1972 Olympics, and the following year became the first woman to run 400 meters in under 50 seconds. In her fourth Olympic appearance in 1977, she improved on her own best time at 400 meters and won another gold. Her hopes for an eighth Olympic medal were ended when a torn tendon caused her to withdraw from competition in 1980. After her stellar athletic career, Irena retired to a quieter life in Poland with her husband, Janusz Szewinska. She became an economist and a sports administrator. In 1998 she was elected to the International Olympic Committee.

Olga Korbut (1956–)
Gymnast

GYMNAST OLGA KORBUT, A NATIVE OF BELARUS, attended one of the Soviet Union's government-sponsored sports schools from the time she was 11. She was 17 when she walked onto the mat at

the 1972 Olympics in Munich, Germany. There she won two gold medals, one silver, and helped to capture the gold medal for team competition. More importantly, this 90-pound "pixie," as she was dubbed by the media, dazzled Olympic audiences with her flexibility and strength, while she performed original and daring moves never before seen in competition. She showed the world the future of her sport, which was soon to be dominated by slender, powerful, young athletes like herself.

Korbut returned to the Olympics in 1976 but was overshadowed by the 15-year-old Romanian Nadia Comaneci. She retired from competition that year, settling in Minsk to work as a coach. Soon after, she married a musician, Leonid Bortkevich, and had a son. In 1986 a nuclear reactor exploded in the nearby town of Chernobyl. Three years later Korbut developed thyroid problems as a result of exposure to the widespread radioactive fallout. She decided to use her fame to call attention to the plight of her people and became spokesperson for the Emergency Help for Children Foundation, an aid organization for victims of the Chernobyl disaster. In 1991 she and her family emigrated to the United States. Today Korbut teaches gymnastics in Atlanta, Georgia, and continues to fund-raise for the sick children in her native country.

Petra Kronberger (1969–)
Skier

IN PETRA KRONBERGER'S NATIVE AUSTRIA, THERE are special schools for gifted skiers. Petra, whose talents were apparent by the age of two, enrolled in such a school when she was ten and began training for what would be a short but spectacular career. Her early hopes were almost dashed, however, when she failed to excel in the sport because of a series of injuries during her teen years. Kronberger didn't give up. By 1988 she had made the Olympic team.

Alpine ski racing includes five different events: slalom, giant slalom, Super G, downhill, and combined. Over the span of about five weeks in late 1990 and early 1991, Kronberger won one competition in each, something that had never been done by a female skier. Unfortunately, she injured her knee in a

fall at the 1991 world championships. She managed to recover enough to compete in 1992, winning her third consecutive World Cup title and two Olympic gold medals in Albertville, France, but the pain was almost unbearable. She announced her retirement soon after, prioritizing her health over a lucrative skiing career.

Julieanne Louise Krone (1963–)
Jockey

JULIE KRONE INHERITED HER LOVE OF HORSES FROM her mother, who trained and rode show horses. She learned to ride before she could walk and won her local county fair horse show in the tiny town of Eau Claire, Michigan, at the age of five. Right after high school, she moved to her grandparents' house in Florida, so she could train as a jockey at the Tampa Bay Downs racetrack. Many horse owners still wouldn't hire a female jockey, even though Krone won or placed often in her races. She traveled to racetracks all over the eastern United States in search of opportunities to ride.

Krone's record grew steadily more impressive. In 1987, with 130 victories at Monmouth Park in New Jersey, she became the first woman to earn a riding title (for most wins in one year) at a major track. The following year, she set a record as the first female jockey to win 1,205 races. At the Belmont Stakes in

1993, she became the first female jockey ever to win a Triple Crown event. Shortly after that, she suffered a serious fall and surprised her doctors by returning to work after only nine months. Still one of the best jockeys riding today, Krone deserves much of the credit for opening the sport to women.

Marion Ladewig (1914–)
Bowler

MICHIGAN NATIVE MARION LADEWIG, ONE OF bowling's biggest superstars, came to the sport relatively late in life. She played softball all through high school. But after she bowled her first round at the Fanatorium in Grand Rapids, she was hooked. In 1949, the first year the Bowling Proprietors' Association of America opened their National All-Star tournament to female competitors, she won. In fact she won the first five All-Stars, scoring higher in 1951 than the men's winner that same year and winning for the last time in 1963, at the age of 48. In 1957 she was the first woman to be named International Bowler of the Year.

Ladewig became quite famous because of the extensive media coverage given to bowling during the 1950s. She was hired by Brunswick-Balke-Collender, an equipment company, to be a consultant and spokesperson. During her 30 years with the company, she attended national and international events, including the 1988 Olympics in Seoul, Korea, where bowling was an exhibition sport for the first time. In 1984 Ladewig became the only bowler ever to be inducted into the International Women's Sports Hall of Fame.

Larissa Latynina (1934–)
Gymnast

IF IT WEREN'T FOR LARISSA LATYNINA, WOMEN'S gymnastics would not be what it is today. She excelled on the uneven parallel bars and the side-horse vault, but her forte was the floor exercise. By introducing balletic choreography and artful transitions into the floor routine, she modernized her sport. Between 1956 and 1964, Latynina competed

in three Olympics and won a total of 18 medals—eight gold, six silver, and four bronze—more than any other athlete, male or female.

Latynina attended the Kiev State Institute of Physical Culture in her native Ukraine. During her competitive career, she married the bicycling champion Yuri Feldman and took time out to have two children. She retired from competition in 1967 after failing to medal in the 1966 World Championships but continued to exert considerable influence. For a decade she was head coach of the Soviet women's gymnastics team, which took the gold medal at the 1972 Olympic Games in Montreal. She then ran her own gymnastics center in Moscow, and during the 1980s she was active as a sports administrator. In 1998 she was inducted into the International Gymnastics Hall of Fame.

Silken Laumann (1965–)
Rower

SILKEN LAUMANN'S BRILLIANT CAREER HAS BEEN fraught with difficulties. After only two years of training in her home province of Ontario, Canada, she won a bronze medal in the double sculls

Elizabeth Le Blond (1861–1934)
Mountaineer

BORN INTO AN ARISTOCRATIC FAMILY IN IRELAND, Elizabeth Hawkins-Whitshed expected to be no more than a charming wife and hostess when she married her first husband, the famous correspondent and traveler Fred Burnaby, in 1878. However, while vacationing in the Swiss Alps three years later, Elizabeth found herself irresistibly drawn to the dazzling snow-covered peaks around her. In the course of that summer, she climbed Mont Blanc—twice—and scaled several lesser mountains, scandalizing her family with her new-found career and sunburned face.

After Burnaby's death in 1885, Elizabeth settled in St. Moritz, Switzerland, with her second husband, J. F. Main. This time she learned to skate and toboggan, and even took up Alpine bicycling and motor car racing. She published a textbook on snow photography and various tourist guidebooks on Spain and Italy, all while pursuing her mountaineering career and establishing a reputation as one of Switzerland's most fashionable hostesses. Elizabeth specialized in winter climbing, which is more challenging than climbing in summer, and she preferred to scale mountains that had never before been climbed in winter. She was widowed again in 1892 and married Aubrey Le Blond eight years later. They traveled together to China, Japan, and Russia. After she retired from climbing, she helped establish the Ladies' Alpine Club in London and served as its president from 1907 until her death.

Lillian Leitzel (1892–1931)
Acrobat, aerialist

BORN INTO A FAMILY OF CIRCUS PERFORMERS IN Breslau, Germany, Leopoldina Alitza Pelikan received formal training in music, dancing, and languages as a child. At the age of 16, she went into the family business.

Using her stage name, Lillian Leitzel, she joined her mother and two aunts in their aerial acrobatic team, the Leamy Ladies. By 1915 she had a top-billed solo act with the Ringling Brothers Circus in the United States. Under the lights of the big top,

competition with her sister, Daniele, at the 1984 Olympics in Los Angeles. But by the following year, she was suffering extreme back pain, because she had been born with a spinal curvature that was aggravated by rowing. She refused to give up, though. In 1991, rowing solo, she won the women's heavyweight division and the 2,000-meter singles race in the World Cup.

She had distinguished herself as one of the world's best female rowers, and she was expected to win the gold in Barcelona, Spain, at the 1992 Summer Olympics. Ten weeks before the games, however, a two-man German scull accidentally rammed her boat. The impact drove a piece of wood into Laumann's leg, injuring her so severely that both men fainted after helping her to safety. Her doctors predicted she would never row again. Through sheer willpower, Laumann returned to her boat before she could walk and raced as planned, miraculously winning a bronze medal. Four years later she won a silver medal at the Olympics in Atlanta, Georgia. She is a Canadian hero for her courage, talent, and determination.

95-pound (43-kg) Lillian was a graceful fairy, though in reality her stunts required tremendous upper-body strength. She was most famous for a maneuver called the "one-arm plange," in which she would hang by her right arm and throw her body up and over her right shoulder, circling like an airplane propeller, as the drum rolled and the spell-bound audience counted the revolutions—often over 100 of them—out loud.

On February 13, 1931, in Copenhagen, the swivel ring on Leitzel's rope broke, and she fell 30 feet (9 m). Although she tried to get up and go on with her performance, she was rushed to the hospital. Once there, she assured her husband, trapeze artist Alfredo Cordona, that she felt fine, but she died of her injuries two days later.

Virginia Holgate Leng (1955–)
Equestrian

VIRGINIA LENG, THE DAUGHTER OF A BRITISH military officer, grew up in a series of exotic places. But wherever she lived—Malta, Cyprus, Singapore, or the Philippines—she always found horses to ride. She claims to have jumped her first fence at the age of three.

Leng's specialty is the three-day event. It begins with dressage, in which the rider directs the horse to perform specific, controlled footwork. Then they navigate a challenging cross-country course. The contest finishes with a round of show jumping. In 1975 Leng was considered a favorite to make the Olympic team, but she fell and crushed her arm during a three-day event competition. It almost had to be amputated. Luckily this proved only a temporary setback, and she was riding competitively again by 1977.

Leng won the European Championships in 1981, 1985, and 1987 and the World Championships in 1982 and 1986. She also finally made it onto the Olympic team, winning an individual bronze medal and a team silver medal at the 1984 games in Los Angeles, and the same again in Seoul in 1988. She is known for the scrupulous care she gives her horses, whose health and safety she values above winning any competition.

Suzanne Rachel Flore Lenglen (1899–1938)
Tennis player

BORN IN COMPIÈGNE, FRANCE, FLAMBOYANT tennis player Suzanne Lenglen dazzled the world with the accuracy of her strokes and her graceful style on the court. She became famous at the age of 15, when she won both the women's singles and doubles titles at the 1914 World Hard-Court Championships in Saint-Cloud, a suburb of Paris.

World War I put competitive tennis on hold, but in 1919 at Wimbledon Lenglen picked up right where she had left off. She also scandalized audiences, wearing a headband and a sleeveless dress that

exposed her calves instead of the traditional corset, long skirt, and sun hat. In the finals, she faced British champion Dorothea Chambers, and they played a grueling 44-game match. Lenglen emerged victorious—and then went on to claim the women's doubles title, too. Her unconventional dress launched a fashion craze and led to a change in women's tennis attire.

Lenglen collected many titles over the next few years, particularly at Wimbledon and at the 1920 Olympics in Antwerp, Belgium. In 1926 she turned professional, then retired from competition in 1927. She wrote several books about tennis, published a few short stories, and founded a tennis school in Paris. Poor health always plagued her: She had suffered childhood asthma, and jaundice had prevented her from playing in 1924. She died at the age of 39, the victim of a blood disorder called pernicious anemia.

Nancy Lieberman-Cline (1958–)
Basketball player

GROWING UP IN BROOKLYN AND QUEENS, NEW York, Nancy Lieberman would join any pickup basketball game she could find. At age 17 she was the youngest player, male or female, ever to be chosen for the United States Olympic team, and in 1979 she helped the U.S. National team win the World Women's Basketball Championship.

In 1981 Lieberman decided to become a professional player when she was recruited by the new

> "I was not allowed to play in the Public School Athletic League because I was a girl, so I found other areas where I was allowed to play. . . . I used to look for any game in any place. I played 'radar ball' at night in the neighborhood playgrounds. There were distant streetlights that gave off a glow, but you could hardly see the basket. But that was fine with me. It helped me develop my shooting touch. Night after night I would practice or play games of one-on-one with my friends."
>
> NANCY LIEBERMAN
> *Basketball My Way,* 1982

Women's Basketball League to play for the Dallas Diamonds. Unfortunately, there just wasn't enough financial support for the sport. Investors didn't believe there was an audience for women's professional basketball. The WBL folded and was replaced by the Women's American Basketball Association. Again, Lieberman played professionally for a year, until the WABA went out of business, too.

After a brief stint as tennis player Martina Navratilova's personal trainer, Lieberman was drafted in 1986 by the U.S. Basketball League and joined the all-male Springfield Fame, a Massachusetts team. She was the first woman ever to play in a male professional league and to earn an equivalent salary. At five feet, ten inches (1.78 m), Lieberman was dwarfed but not dominated by the men. After two seasons, she joined the Washington Generals, the team that tours with the Harlem Globetrotters, and married a teammate, Tim Cline. The establishment of the newest women's professional league, the WNBA, brought her back from a busy retirement. After playing a season for the Phoenix Mercury, she accepted a position as coach of the Detroit Shock in 1998.

Tara Lipinski (1982–)
Figure skater

TARA LIPINSKI, QUICK ON HER FEET SINCE THE unusually early age of six months, started roller skating at age three and ice skating at six. It was soon obvious that she had talent, so in 1993 Tara and her mother went to Delaware to train, while her father stayed with his job as an oil executive in Texas.

Lipinski's dedication paid off early. At age 12 she became the youngest female winner ever in the Olympic Sports Festival, a showcase for up-and-coming American athletes. In 1996 she successfully performed two consecutive triple-loop jumps in competition, something no woman had done before. By then her greatest rival was the American favorite, Michelle Kwan. But Lipinski consistently demonstrated her merit. In 1997 she won the United States national championship *and* the world championship, then went on to take the gold at the 1998 Olympics in Nagano, Japan. Shortly thereafter she gave up her amateur status by skating in, and winning, a professional event in South Carolina.

Rebecca Lobo (1973–)
Basketball player

REBECCA LOBO DESERVES A LOT OF THE CREDIT FOR winning Americans over to women's basketball. Wherever she plays, she attracts crowds of fans. During her high school career in Southwick, Massachusetts, Lobo earned 2,710 points—more than any other player, male or female, in the history of Massachusetts high-school basketball.

Many colleges competed for her attention, but the six-foot, four-inch Lobo chose the University of Connecticut, less than an hour away from her family home. She helped the UConn Huskies win two consecutive Big East Conference championships, and in 1995, her senior year, they won the NCAA championship. The games drew unprecedented numbers of spectators, a phenomenon that her fans dubbed "Lobo fever." Lobo graduated on the dean's list with a degree in political science. Then she became the youngest member of the United States Olympic women's basketball team, which won the gold medal at the summer games in Atlanta. Since 1996 Lobo has been playing professionally in the newly formed WNBA for the New York Liberty.

Jeannie Longo (1958–)
Cyclist

JEANNIE LONGO'S FIRST SPORT WAS SKIING, BUT when she didn't make the French national team in 1979, she switched to cycling. It turned out to be a good move. In her first season she became the French road racing champion and retained that title for the next ten years.

Bad luck plagued Longo in her first two Olympic competitions. She finally won a silver medal in the road race at the 1992 Olympics, but the gold eluded her until 1996. However, she captured just about every other title along the way, including the women's Tour de France three times and a total of 11 world championships.

A loner with a single-minded drive to win, Longo has been called arrogant and unsportsmanlike. Although the same sort of aggressive attitude is unremarkable in male athletes, it has made her unpopular. No one denies her awesome talent, though, and many people consider her the greatest female racer of all time. Now past 40, Longo has announced her retirement more than once—but so far she continues to race. She lives in Grenoble with her husband and coach, Patrice Ciprelli.

Nancy Lopez (1957–)
Golfer

WHEN CALIFORNIA NATIVE NANCY LOPEZ'S parents took up golfing for exercise, she used to follow them around the course. Then one day her father let her try hitting the ball and realized how talented she was. While still at high school in New Mexico, Lopez won junior titles and tied for second in the U.S. Women's Open. In 1977 she left college to become a professional golfer. Within a year she was a national celebrity, winning nine titles on the Ladies' Professional Golf Association (LPGA) tour.

Lopez married professional baseball player Ray Knight in 1982 and had three daughters over the next nine years, which required her to structure her career around the needs of her young family. She remained a dominant force among professional golfers, though. In 1985 she set a record for her season scoring average and earned $400,000, more than anyone else on the women's circuit. She is known for the strength of her long drives, her accurate putting, and her poise. Her numerous awards and honors include being named the Associated Press's Female Athlete of the Year in 1978 and 1985 and membership in the LPGA Hall of Fame since 1987. Still extremely popular with golf fans everywhere, Lopez continues to play with the LPGA.

Floretta Doty McCutcheon
(1888–1967)
Bowler

W HEN FLORETTA McCUTCHEON WAS 35, HER husband, Robert, enrolled her in a bowling league without her knowledge. Three years later she was a local sensation in her home state of Colorado and had started bowling in exhibitions. In 1927 she beat world-champion bowler Jimmy Smith in a challenge match that made national headlines. An equipment company offered her a position as a traveling instructor the following year. She accepted

it to help pay for her daughter's college education, but she also discovered that she loved teaching.

For ten years McCutcheon toured the country, teaching women and children how to bowl during the day and playing in exhibition matches at night. She gave special instruction to high school girls, blind bowlers, and female college students. During her career McCutcheon's average score was an impressive 201, and she bowled ten "perfect" games, in which she achieved the highest possible score of 300. After 1938 she settled in New York City and, later, Chicago, where she continued to teach and organize women's leagues. She is credited with attracting thousands of women to the sport with her enthusiasm, talent, and gracious manner. She was inducted into the Women's International Bowling Congress Hall of Fame in 1956 and the Colorado Sports Hall of Fame in 1973.

Heather McKay (1941–)
Squash and racquetball player

A T THE HEIGHT OF HER COMPETITIVE SQUASH career, Heather McKay was truly unbeatable. In 20 years she lost only two matches, and both those defeats came during her first two years in the sport. Male and female players alike consider her the greatest squash player of all time. But squash wasn't her only talent.

McKay grew up in an athletic family near Canberra, Australia. The eighth of 11 children, Heather and her siblings played tennis, field hockey, and cricket. By age 16 she was the local women's tennis champion, as well as the best field hockey player on her high school and town teams. She took up squash to stay in shape for hockey when she was 18 and soon was winning regional championships.

In 1960, with less than a year's experience, McKay won the Australian national tournament. She went on to win 14 Australian national titles, 16 consecutive British Opens, and the only two world championships held during her career. She and her husband, Brian McKay, moved to Canada in 1975. Four years later, looking for a new challenge, she took up racquetball. By 1980 she was Canada's racquetball champion, a title she held until she retired from competition and returned home to Australia in 1985.

Ella Kini Maillart (1903–1997)
Explorer, writer

Swiss-born Ella Maillart was an athlete, a writer, and an intrepid traveler. She represented her country in the 1924 Olympics as a sailor, skied competitively for three years, and was the captain of the Swiss women's ice hockey team in 1931. She dabbled in archaeology in Greece and film production in Moscow. But she never stayed in one place for long. For several decades Maillart traveled nearly nonstop, writing in both French and English about her perilous adventures and the political and social issues she encountered.

She began her travels in the early 1920s, when she went to Russia to study the effects of the 1917 revolution. In 1934, by then a journalist for the newspaper *Petit Parisien*, Maillart traveled an extraordinary 3,500 miles (5,632 km) across China and into northern India with fellow writer Peter Fleming, covering much of the distance on foot or horseback. Her book, *Oasis interdites* (1937, published in English as *Forbidden Journey*), describes that adventure. In 1939 she drove her car from France to Afghanistan, then spent most of World War II in southern India. She was one of the first westerners to explore Nepal when its borders opened in 1949, an experience she documented in *The Land of the Sherpas* (1955). In the 1950s Maillart hiked in the Himalayas and explored Tibet. Even after "retiring" to her chalet in Chandolin, Switzerland, she worked as a travel guide for many years.

Beryl Markham (1902–1986)
Aviator, adventurer, writer

When Beryl Markham was a toddler, her father brought her to Africa, where she grew up in the hills outside Nairobi, Kenya. The spirited British girl learned to speak fluent Swahili and Masai, and became proficient at such skills as hunting wild pigs. She apprenticed in her father's business as a horse breeder and trainer, and when he moved on to Peru in 1919, she decided to stay in her adopted homeland.

Markham not only earned her racehorse trainer's license, she also became a commercial pilot. She was a highly visible member of the aristocratic white

community in Africa, admired for her beauty and poise. In 1936 Markham made the first-ever transatlantic solo flight from east to west. After spending 21 hours and 25 minutes *en route* from England, she crash-landed in Nova Scotia. Afterward she moved to Hollywood, California, and published her acclaimed memoir, *West with the Night* (1942). Ernest Hemingway raved about the book. However, many doubted Markham was capable of writing such beautiful prose and suggested that her husband, screenwriter Raoul Schumacher, was responsible for it. If so, he made no public attempt to claim authorship. After World War II, Markham returned to Nairobi to train horses and lived there as an eccentric recluse until her death.

Christy Martin (1968–)
Boxer

Christy Salters started boxing on a dare. She was a freshman basketball player at Concord College in her native West Virginia when friends urged her to enter a local "Toughwoman" contest. She knew nothing about boxing, but as it turned out, the sport excited her and suited her naturally assertive nature—she won the $1,000 first prize.

Christy graduated from college in three years with honors and a degree in education. Then she found a trainer, Jim Martin, and started competing whenever she could (they married in 1992). She signed a contract with promoter Don King in 1993, becoming the only woman on his roster of famous clients. In 1996 she fought in the first women's match to be broadcast live on national television. A month later, wearing her trademark pink trunks, she defeated Deirdre Gogarty in the World Boxing Council's women's championship. Over one million television viewers tuned in. With nearly 40 wins and only two losses on her record, Christy Martin is the world's most famous female boxer, and one of the best.

Leslie Marx (1967–)
Fencer

LESLIE MARX HAS BECOME PROFICIENT AT JUGGLING dual careers. She is not only a world-class fencer, but she is also an assistant professor of economics at the University of Rochester, New York.

Pan American Games

The Pan American Games, an Olympics-style competition that is held every four years, brings together athletes from the Americas and the Caribbean. The idea was introduced in 1940, and an initial planning meeting was held in Buenos Aires, Argentina. However, the outbreak of World War II delayed the first competition until 1951. That year, 2,000 athletes representing 20 countries took part in 19 sporting events, and it was a decided success. By 1999, those numbers had more than doubled. Approximately 5,000 athletes from 42 nations competed in 41 different sports. Leslie Marx's event, women's fencing, has been a part of the Pan American games since the very beginning.

The two pursuits go together well, though. An average épée bout lasts nine minutes; it calls for strategy and—Marx's academic specialty—a sophisticated knowledge of game theory.

Marx, a native Texan, was introduced to fencing when she was a college student at Duke University. She had signed up for fencing classes to fulfill a physical education requirement, but she quickly came to love it. Intrigued by its intellectual as well as its physical challenge, she showed so much promise that she was recruited by the school's fencing team. In 1993 she won her first of two national épée championships, and in 1995 she earned the gold medal at the Pan American Games. At the 1996 Olympics in Atlanta, Georgia, Marx placed 16th in the individual épée competition, an impressive showing for an American in a sport where Europeans dominate. Now the top-ranked American épée fencer, she continues to combine athletic competition and teaching in her busy life.

Vera Menchik-Stevenson (1906–1944)
Chess player

ALTHOUGH HER FATHER WAS CZECH AND HER mother was English, Vera Menchik was born in Russia. She spent her first 15 years there, learning how to play chess from her father. In 1921 she moved to England to study under the grand master

Géza Maróczy. With her strong, conservative tactical style, Vera was soon a dominant player in women's chess, winning the first Women's World Championship tournament, which was held in London in 1927. She also competed against male players, sometimes taking second or third place in British men's tournaments. She became a grand master and retained her women's championship title through six consecutive tournaments, until World War II temporarily brought an end to international competition.

A fun-loving woman, Menchik was respected for her sportsmanship and lack of pretension. She married R. H. Stevenson in 1937 and became an adopted British citizenship. Vera, her mother, and her sister were killed in 1944, when their London home was destroyed in an air raid. She was 38 years old.

Shannon Miller (1977–)
Gymnast

WHEN SHANNON MILLER WAS FIVE YEARS OLD, she received a trampoline for Christmas. She loved the gift and spent lots of time jumping on it and figuring out tricks. In fact, her daring flips and twists on the toy frightened her parents so much that they took her to gymnastics classes, where she could learn to do such things safely. Shannon soon proved to be a talented gymnast. When she attended a gymnastics camp in the former Soviet Union at age nine, she was inspired by the Soviet athletes' work ethic. She started training in earnest when she returned home to Edmond, Oklahoma.

In 1990, at age 13, Miller made the United States gymnastics team. Two years later in Barcelona, Spain, she won no fewer than five Olympic medals, two silver and three bronze. By 1994 she had won seven world championship medals, more than any other American gymnast. Miller decided to make the 1996 Atlanta Olympics her last. By then she was 19—ancient by gymnastics standards. Still, she brought home an individual gold medal on the balance beam and helped her team to win the gold. Having graduated from high school in 1994 with straight As, Miller went on to attend the University of Oklahoma after retiring from competition.

Virne Beatrice "Jackie" Mitchell (1914–1987)
Baseball player

BEFORE SOFTBALL WAS DEEMED MORE FEMININE, women played baseball. One of the best players was Jackie Mitchell, a phenomenal left-handed—or "southpaw"—pitcher. After performing well in amateur games, Mitchell was offered a contract with her hometown's minor league team, the Chattanooga Lookouts, in 1931.

Signing with the Lookouts at the tender age of 17, Mitchell became only the second woman ever to join a men's professional baseball team. A few weeks later, the New York Yankees came to Tennessee to play an exhibition game. That day Mitchell faced baseball greats Babe Ruth and Lou Gehrig and struck them *both* out, making national headlines. Although some sportswriters contended that the two batting legends must have missed on purpose, several members of the New York team denied it. Mitchell never got the chance to prove her doubters wrong, though. Baseball Commissioner Kenesaw Landis soon

announced that the game was too rough for women and voided Mitchell's contract. She went on to play in exhibition games with non-league teams and retired in 1937.

Rosi Mittermaier (1950–)
Skier

ROSI MITTERMAIER WAS BORN IN REIT IM WINKEL, a town in the German Alps where skiing was a part of everyday life. Her father operated a ski school. Rosi and her sisters, Evi and Heidi, all became members of the national ski team.

In 1967 Rosi competed for the first World Cup, a title awarded to skiers based on their records in a season-long series of races. For nine years she competed in every event category (slalom, giant slalom, and downhill). After 1968 she consistently placed among the top 15 in World Cup rankings. She was a solid, but not a first-rate, competitor. Her Olympic experience in 1968 was disappointing; in her best race she finished 20th. At the Olympics four years later, her performance improved, but not enough to earn a medal.

It wasn't until the 1976 Olympics in Innsbruck, Austria, that Mittermaier became a champion

overnight. She woke up on the morning of her first race having dreamed that she would win—and she proceeded to place first in both the downhill and the slalom. In the giant slalom competition, she missed winning by only a fraction of a second. A joyous Mittermaier returned home with two golds and one silver medal. She was a national heroine. After retiring from competition that year, she married a teammate, Christian Neureuther.

Helen Wills Moody (1905–1998)
Tennis player

ALWAYS A DETERMINED PERFECTIONIST, HELEN Wills won her first United States national title at age 17, only three years after she picked up a tennis racket for the first time. The impressive career that followed included six more United States singles titles, eight Wimbledon singles championships, four French singles titles, and two gold medals at the 1924 Paris Olympics. From 1927 to 1932, she never lost a set in a singles match.

Uninhibited by the social standards of her day, Wills felt that binding clothing handicapped the player, both mentally and physically. She joined the French tennis player Suzanne Lenglen in liberating

her sport from its confining dress code. Her standard outfit included a knee-length skirt, a sleeveless top, and a white visor.

Wills met her first husband, Frederick Moody, in 1926, a few minutes after losing a much-publicized exhibition match with Lenglen. After divorcing Frederick in 1937, she married Aidan Roark, a polo player and screenwriter. She also pursued many interests outside tennis. While establishing her sports career, Moody had also earned a degree in fine arts from the University of California in her hometown of Berkeley. She went on to write and illustrate articles for the *Saturday Evening Post*, publish two books about tennis, and coauthor a mystery novel, *Death Serves an Ace* (1939). On several occasions she exhibited her paintings in New York galleries. Moody continued to play recreational tennis until she was 82 years old.

Annemarie Moser-Proell (1953–)
Skier

As a child Annemarie Proell skied in the Austrian mountains near her family's farm whenever she could. Her father carved her first pair of wooden skis for her. From then on Annemarie was fearless on every hill, even though she never had any formal training.

By the time she was 17, she dominated the slopes as an alpine ski racer. In 1971 she won the overall World Cup title for the first of five consecutive times, a record. She won two silver medals in the 1972 Olympics; those second-place finishes left her bitterly disappointed.

By 1976 Proell had tired of the pressures of racing. Retiring from competitive skiing, she married soccer player Herbert Moser and opened a café. But she found herself still attracted to the slopes, so she returned to competition in 1979 and won the World Cup for the sixth time. In 1980, at age 27, Moser-Proell was considered too old for competitive alpine skiing. Determined to earn an Olympic gold medal at last, she ignored the skeptics. She won the downhill race in Lake Placid, New York, and then retired for good. Her record for most World Cup titles still stands—in fact no one, man or woman, has managed to equal it yet.

Rosa Mota (1958–)
Long-distance runner

Rosa Mota was 16 years old when she entered a high-school race on a whim and won. She enjoyed it so much she continued to run, despite being jeered at by men on the streets of her hometown of Oporto, Portugal. They simply weren't used to seeing girls exercise.

In 1982 Mota went to the European Championship competition in Athens as a competitor in the 3,000-meter race. While there, she insisted upon entering the women's marathon as well, and she surprised everyone by winning. No Portuguese athlete had won a gold medal in the European Championships before, and Rosa became an instant heroine back home. Other victories followed, including three European Championship marathons (in 1982, 1986, and 1990), three Boston Marathons (in 1987, 1988, and 1990), the 1987 World Championship in Rome, and the women's marathon at the 1988 Olympics in Seoul.

Starting in 1989 various health problems kept Rosa out of international competition. However, by 1994 she was back in shape and entering races, although in a more limited way. She also started a second career: In 1995 she was elected to the Portuguese Parliament, a position she still holds. Mota is known for her outgoing personality, her commitment to helping young runners, and her longevity as a world-class marathoner.

Nawal el-Moutawakel (1962–)
Runner

Nawal el-Moutawakel lives in Morocco, an Islamic country where women are discouraged from participating in sports. Luckily for Nawal, her father supported her as mentor and coach, but her career was disrupted twice by tragedy.

El-Moutawakel received an athletic scholarship to Iowa State University, and shortly after she arrived in America, her father died. The following year she skipped an out-of-town meet because she needed to study. The plane carrying her teammates crashed, killing everyone aboard. Despite these setbacks, she won the women's 400-meter hurdles in the 1984

Olympic Games in Los Angeles. It was the first time that race was included in the Olympics, and she was the first Moroccan and first Islamic woman to win an Olympic medal. Her victory in Los Angeles took place in the middle of the night in her hometown of Casablanca, where the streets immediately filled with triumphant revelers. El-Moutawakel retired to fulfill her traditional Muslim role of wife and mother—but with a difference. She is also a sports writer, a track coach, and an active promoter of women's sports in Africa.

Shirley Muldowney (1940–)
Drag racer

S HIRLEY ROQUE WAS 14 WHEN JACK MULDOWNEY taught her to drive in his souped-up 1951 Mercury. Soon she was racing late at night on the streets of Schenectady, New York. Shirley and Jack married in 1956, and with Jack as her mechanic, she

set out to break into the male-only sport of professional drag racing, a quarter-mile race between two cars. Muldowney encountered widespread sexism, her marriage failed, and she had some close brushes with death, but she became one of the sport's most famous drivers.

In 1965 Muldowney was the first woman to be licensed by the National Hot Rod Association. She won her first NHRA title in 1976, and the next year she became the first racer ever to win three consecutive events for Top Fuel cars, a specially designed model for drag racing. She also set her share of speed records, such as her 1983 velocity of 257.87 miles per hour (415 kph). That same year Hollywood filmmakers released a movie about her life, *Heart Like a Wheel.*

In 1984 Muldowney was injured in a serious crash at the Grand Nationals in Montreal. However, after five surgeries, she returned to racing her signature hot-pink car in 1986. She still hasn't announced her retirement.

Lucille Mulhall (1875–1940)
Rodeo star

L UCILLE MULHALL IS REMEMBERED AS AMERICA'S original "cowgirl." Growing up on an 80,000-acre (32,375-ha) ranch in Oklahoma, she learned to ride and rope alongside her brothers. It was apparent from a very early age that she possessed talent as a ranch hand. Her father, Colonel Zach Mulhall, told a seven-year-old Lucy that he would give her all the calves she could tie and brand herself. Before long two-thirds of his stock belonged to his daughter.

As a teenager she toured with her father's Wild West Show, which also featured Will Rogers. In 1901 she and the show's cowboy band led the parade at the inauguration of President William McKinley and Vice-President Theodore Roosevelt, an old family friend. The next year, in El Paso, Texas, Lucy competed in her first steer-roping contest. When it became clear that she had won, the spectators stormed the field and tried to rip her clothes off—they didn't believe she was female. She was, in fact, the first woman to compete against men, and she broke the world record for steer roping twice.

Mulhall also appeared in variety shows. Billed as "America's Greatest Horsewoman" or the "Queen of the Range," she performed horseback-riding stunts and cowboy rope tricks for wildly enthusiastic audiences. Eventually, she retired from show business and went to live on her father's Oklahoma ranch. She was 65 years old when she was killed in a car accident.

Aimee Mullins (1976–)
Sprinter

IT TAKES A LOT TO SLOW AIMEE MULLINS DOWN. Because she was born without fibulas (important weight-bearing bones) in her calves, her legs were amputated just below the knee when she was a year old. Despite this, she learned to walk on prosthetic legs at age two and grew up playing softball and soccer with the rest of the kids in her Allentown, Pennsylvania, neighborhood.

A recent graduate of the Georgetown University School of Foreign Service, Mullins started training in track and field in 1995. At the 1996 Paralympics in Atlanta, Georgia, she entered three events—the long jump and the 100-meter and 200-meter dashes—and set records for the double amputee class in the first two. She wasn't able to win a medal, though, because Paralympic rules require certain numbers of athletes from different countries to compete in each race. In all three events she ran against women who were arm amputees and still had both legs.

Mullins continues to train, her sights set on the 2000 Paralympics in Sydney, Australia. But she has also become well known for her efforts to change social attitudes about beauty and what it means to be differently abled. She works closely with designers to create better prosthetic limbs for herself and others, and she has challenged the world of high fashion with her work as a model.

Margaret Murdock (1942–)
Sharpshooter

KANSAS NATIVE MARGARET MURDOCK HOLDS A remarkable and historic record. In 1967, at the Pan American Games, Murdock achieved a score of 391 in the small-bore rifle competition, setting a world record and, more notably, making her the first female athlete ever to surpass a men's record in any sport.

Perhaps because sharpshooting doesn't draw large crowds, the news media made little of the event. However, nine years later Murdock again proved her ability to compete on the same level as men. In the small-bore, three-position competition at the Olympic Games in Montreal, she and her male teammate Lanny Bassham tied for first place. Bassham received the gold medal because of a rules technicality, but as *The Star-spangled Banner* played during the awards ceremony, he reached down and pulled Murdock up to join him at the top level of the victory platform.

With several other national and international small-bore rifle championships under her belt, Murdock is considered one of the best sharpshooters of her time. She is also a registered nurse who specializes in anesthesiology. In 1988 she was inducted into the International Women's Sports Hall of Fame.

Dervla Murphy (1931–)
Traveler, writer

IT IS RARE, IN THE LATE 20TH CENTURY, TO FIND A traveler similar to those intrepid 19th-century English ladies who set out to walk, canoe, or ride a slow animal through vast, untouristed lands. Dervla Murphy is just such a rare adventurer.

> **"Many hours on the sand-dunes had been spent methodically planning my journey to India. Having for the past twenty years intended to make this journey, it did not strike me as in any way an odd idea. I thought then, as I still do, that if someone enjoys cycling and wishes to go to India, the obvious thing is to cycle there. Soon, however, I realised that most people were regarding me either as a lunatic or an embryonic heroine; in 1962 Western youth's mass trek to the East had not yet begun."**
>
> DERVLA MURPHY
> *Wheels Within Wheels,* 1979

Born in County Waterford, Ireland, Murphy spent her childhood writing adventure stories. At the age of 14 she was forced to quit school to take care of her mother, who suffered from rheumatoid arthritis. After the deaths of both her parents, she found herself, at age 30, free to travel. Her first trip was the fulfillment of a childhood dream: bicycling across Europe, through the Middle East, and into India. She also traveled to Tibet, Nepal, Ethiopia, and the Andes, accompanied only by her bicycle or a mule named Jock.

After her daughter, Rachel, was born in 1968, Murphy at last found a human traveling companion who suited her. Together they have shared many adventures, including a trip to southern India when Rachel was five, and a jaunt into the West African tropics in 1987. In addition to her informative and humorous travel books, such as *In Ethiopia with a Mule* (1968) and *Muddling Through in Madagascar* (1985), Murphy has written about her native Ireland and the nuclear arms race.

Martina Navratilova (1956–)
Tennis player

MARTINA NAVRATILOVA WAS BORN INTO A TENNIS playing family. Growing up in Revnice, Czechoslovakia, she started taking tennis lessons at age six and by her early teens was her country's top player. The Communist government managed her career with a heavy hand, however. In 1975 Navratilova defected to America, and she became a citizen six years later.

Navratilova earned her first number one world ranking in 1978, and for the next 13 years, she ranked among the world's top three players. One reason for Navratilova's dominance was that she embarked on a regime of weight lifting, running, and eating well. This conditioning, which was rare for female athletes at the time, gave her a muscular physique and a definite edge over her opponents. In all, she won 54 Grand Slam events, including nine Wimbledon, four U.S. Open, three Australian, and two French Open singles championships, as well as numerous doubles and mixed-doubles competitions. She also engaged in a world-famous rivalry with American tennis great Chris Evert that lasted for ten years.

Since retiring from professional competition in 1994, Navratilova has devoted her considerable

energy to promoting women's athletics and lesbian and gay rights in professional sports. The recipient of numerous awards, she was inducted into the International Women's Sports Hall of Fame in 1984.

Paula Newby-Fraser (1962–)
Triathlete

Born in Harare, Zimbabwe, and raised in South Africa, Paula Newby-Fraser has been called the "Empress of Endurance." It's a fitting title. Her sport is the triathlon, a grueling test of athletic versatility that consists of a 2.4-mile (4-km) swim, a 112-mile (180-km) cycling course, and a 26.2-mile (42-km) run.

As a child she excelled at swimming and ballet, but during her teens she stopped participating in sports. After graduating from college in 1984, Paula started jogging to lose weight. She entered her first triathlon in 1985, without ever having run 26 miles in one day and only eight weeks after buying a bicycle. She didn't just win: She set a new women's record and finished in the top ten overall. Newby-Fraser moved to southern California to train in earnest, and in 1986 she won her first Hawaii Ironman Triathlon, the sport's top event. She has since won it a record eight times. In 1992 she finished in 8 hours, 55 minutes, and 28 seconds, a world record that has yet to be broken.

Newby-Fraser has received numerous endorsement contracts and was named Professional Athlete of the Year in 1990 by the Women's Sports Foundation. In 1996 she became a United States citizen. Having won over 20 triathlons in her career, Newby-Fraser has begun to consider retiring. She now writes about fitness and promotes her sport.

Annie Oakley (Phoebe Ann Moses) (1860–1926)
Sharpshooter

Annie Oakley is a true American legend. Remembered as "the Girl of the Western Plains" clad in a cowboy hat and fringe, she could shoot better than almost any man. Born Phoebe Ann Moses, in Darke County, Ohio, she taught herself

to use a gun before she was ten. In her early teens, she paid off a debt that threatened her family's house by hunting quail and pheasant for Cincinnati restaurants, earning their highest rate for birds shot cleanly through the head.

In 1876 Phoebe married sharpshooter Frank Butler, who taught her how to read and write. Together they developed an act, for which she adopted her famous stage name. In 1885 "Butler and Oakley" signed on with Buffalo Bill Cody's Wild West Show, featuring rodeo cowboys and Indians from the "Old West." Annie became the main attraction, shooting glass balls in midair while standing on the back of a galloping horse or riddling a playing card with bullets from a distance of 30 yards (27 m). Despite her rowdy image, Oakley was soft-spoken offstage, reading or doing needlework in her tent between shows.

Oakley spent nearly 15 years with Buffalo Bill but left in 1901 after being injured in a train crash. She spent time as an actress, then began giving

shooting demonstrations and lessons to wealthy society women. A car accident in 1922 left her partially paralyzed; she died four years later. However, she became famous all over again in 1946, when *Annie Get Your Gun*, the stage musical based on her life, opened on Broadway.

Okamoto Ayako (1951–)
Golfer

OKAMOTO AYAKO, A NATIVE OF HIROSHIMA, Japan, started out her athletic career by playing softball. As an employee at the Yamato Textile Company, she joined the company team and quickly made a name for herself as one of Japan's best pitchers. Eventually, though, she discovered that she was more interested in golf. Having taken up the sport at the age of 23, she went on to win 20 Japanese national golf tournaments and become a superstar in her country.

In 1982, eager to compete against the world's best players, Okamoto moved to the United States. She was soon one of the top players in the Ladies Professional Golf Association. In 1987 she was the first foreign-born golfer to be named Player of the Year by the LPGA. That year she won a place in the *Guinness Book of World Records*, shooting 17 under par during a three-day tournament. In addition to winning 17 LPGA events, she has won several international titles, including the 1986 British Open. Okamoto still plays professionally, primarily in Japan, which she once again calls home. She is also the designer of the Wakasu Golf Links, near downtown Tokyo.

Micheline Ostermeyer (1922–)
Track-and-field athlete

MICHELINE OSTERMEYER, A FRENCHWOMAN WHO grew up in Tunisia, was not only a talented athlete but a gifted musician as well. In 1946, while she was enrolled as a student at the Paris Conservatory of Music, she placed second in the shot-put competition at the European Track and Field Championships. Two years later she graduated with high honors, ready to begin her career as a concert pianist.

At the time the 1948 Olympic Games were just three months away, and the French track-and-field team was eager to find a good competitor for the discus throw. They begged Ostermeyer to take on the challenge. Four coaches helped her to train with the discus, because she had only thrown it in competition once before. Her performance at the games in London was spectacular. She won the discus throw and the shot put, and she claimed the bronze medal for the high jump.

Ostermeyer continued to compete as an athlete until 1951, when an injury forced her to retire. She then went back to the musical career she had originally planned, performing in concerts and becoming a music teacher.

Mary Ewing Outerbridge (1852–1886)
Tennis player

MANY PEOPLE ATTRIBUTE THE INTRODUCTION OF tennis in the United States to Mary Outerbridge, a Philadelphia-born socialite who lived on Staten Island, New York. Even if she wasn't the very first person to bring the sport to the country, her enthusiasm certainly helped to make it a widely played and well-loved game.

Lawn tennis was invented by an Englishman, Major Walter Clopton, in 1873. Outerbridge encountered the game when it was still very new, perhaps as early as 1874. She was vacationing in Bermuda, and the English tourists there taught her to play. Eager to enjoy the sport at home, too, she carried rackets, balls, and a net back on the boat. She installed a court at the Staten Island Cricket and Baseball Club, where she and her family were prominent members. It didn't take long to catch on.

A talented player, Mary won tournaments and helped found a women's tennis organization. She died at age 34 after a three-year illness, but her older brother Eugenius continued to promote and support the sport by sponsoring men's championships at the club. Mary was inducted into the Tennis Hall of Fame in 1981.

Denise Parker (1973–)
Archer

IN A SPORT WHERE ATHLETES TEND TO DO BETTER the older and bigger they are, 90-pound Denise Parker surprised experts when she entered the world of competitive archery at the age of 13. The following year her home state of Utah lowered its age requirement for obtaining a bow-hunting license from 16 to 14 just for Parker, who had returned with a team bronze medal from the 1988 Olympic Games in Seoul, Korea.

Denise first picked up a bow at age ten. It wasn't long before she was invited onto the *Tonight Show* to shoot an arrow through a Lifesaver candy. Between 1988 and 1995, she won the National Indoor Championship every year but one. She was the youngest-ever winner of the individual gold medal in her sport at the 1987 Pan American Games, and she repeated that victory in 1991. At the 1995 Pan American Games, her participation was critical to her team's gold-medal performance.

Parker is currently the editor of *Archery Focus*, the magazine of the National Archery Association. She continues to compete as a member of the U.S. national team—and, because archery is a lifetime sport, there is no telling how far she could still go.

Annie Smith Peck (1850–1935)
Mountain climber

ANNIE SMITH PECK, A SCHOLAR FROM RHODE Island, began climbing relatively late in life. She was the first woman student at the American School of Classical Studies in Athens, Greece, and after returning home in 1886, she taught Latin and gave lectures. But she had become fascinated by the Swiss Matterhorn while she was abroad.

By 1895 she had left academia, secured funding, and become the third woman to stand atop the Matterhorn. Dozens of climbs followed. In 1887 she tackled Popocatépetl and Mount Orizaba, both in Mexico. Peck's trips were often financed by publications such as the *New York World*, for which she wrote accounts of her adventures. Her fame led to a rivalry with another great woman climber, Fanny Bullock Workman.

In 1903 Peck began climbing South American peaks. After two failed efforts to scale Mount Illampu in Bolivia, she heard that Mount Huascarán in the Peruvian Andes was taller. It took five attempts, but she conquered Huascarán in 1908, at 58 years old. She thought she had achieved a world record—until Workman sent surveyors to measure the mountain. It turned out she had climbed 21,812 feet (6,650 m),

a record only for the Western Hemisphere, but one that held for 26 years.

Peck was also an active suffragist. In 1911 she planted a banner that read "Votes for Women" on Mount Coropuna in Peru. She continued to travel and write well into her 80s.

Ida Pfeiffer (1797–1858)
Traveler

It wasn't until she was middle aged that Austrian native Ida Pfeiffer was able to pursue her dream of traveling alone around the world. As a young woman, she had consented to marry a lawyer who was 25 years her senior, and their marriage had been lukewarm at best. By 1842 they were living apart, their sons were grown, and Pfeiffer set out to see the world beyond Vienna. She ignored her friends' disapproval and her lack of money, financing her adventures by writing books about them.

Pfeiffer ventured alone into the Holy Land, Iceland, Brazil, China, India, Iraq, Russia, and many other places. She spent several months living with two separate cannibal tribes, the Dyaks of Borneo and the Batak of Sumatra, and was the first westerner to report on their cultures. In a final excursion to Madagascar in 1857, she was imprisoned for a time by the hostile Queen Ranavalona and contracted a serious illness, which caused her death a year later.

It is clear from her books that Ida Pfeiffer was often intolerant of other cultures and ethnicities.

> "The greater part of this journey through the wilderness I was compelled to walk barefoot, as it is impossible, when you have not only morasses, but also water to walk through, to find any kind of *chaussure* [footwear], that will answer the purpose. . . . At the end of every day's journey I was obliged to get one of the natives to pull out the thorns. . . . Very often my feet were so sore, that I thought I could not possibly go on on the following morning, but when the time came I always did."
>
> Ida Pfeiffer, on her trek through Sumatra
> *A Lady's Second Journey Around the World*, 1856

Despite her critical views of non-Europeans, however, she did courageously blaze a trail of independent travel, and she managed to do it at a time when women were rarely independent.

Judit Polgar (1976–)
Chess player

Judit Polgar and her older sisters, Zsuzsa and Zsofia, were groomed from birth by their psychologist father to be geniuses. Judit learned to play chess at age four and, like her sisters (who are also top players), trained seven hours a day with the help of professional coaches. At age 15 she became the youngest person, and only the fourth woman, ever to earn the title of grand master by defeating ten grand masters in succession at the Hungarian Super Championships in Budapest.

In 1993 Polgar played a ten-game exhibition match against former world champion Boris Spassky and defeated him, winning $110,000 in the process. Some chess traditionalists predict that there will never be a female world champion. They believe that women lack natural aggression and are incapable of sustaining a prolonged battle. So far, Polgar has proved them wrong, and her career is far from over. Her style of play has been called "ferocious," and she has intimidated many older, more experienced male players. She could one day be a world champion.

Marjorie Pollard (1899–1982)
Field hockey player

Marjorie Pollard was one of the most extraordinary field hockey players England ever produced. When she first started playing at school, she tended goal, but soon she switched to playing forward, where her scoring talent was allowed to shine.

Pollard played for England's national field hockey team for most of the 1920s and 1930s. In 1926, in a match against Germany, she scored every single goal for her team, leading them to an 8–0 victory. Two years later, she scored 13 goals in England's 20–0 defeat of the Welsh team. She also played on local teams around Peterborough, Northampton-shire, where she was born. After many years of playing for the Peterborough club, she founded the North Northants team. Cricket was another sport she excelled at; she helped to found the England Women's Cricket Association.

Pollard played her last game in 1949 and went on to become president of the All England Women's Hockey Association. She also worked as a sports journalist for British papers such as the *Times*, *Guardian*, and *Morning Post*. For nearly 25 years, until she was 80 years old, she edited a publication called *Hockey Field*.

Harriet Quimby (1875–1912)
Aviator

Flamboyant Harriet Quimby claimed to have been born in 1884 to a well-off California family, although historians suspect she was nearly ten years older and the daughter of a Michigan farmer. However, she did grow up in California, where she became a drama critic and a journalist for magazines and newspapers.

In 1903 she moved to New York City to write for *Leslie's Weekly*, and it was there that she became interested in flying. She enrolled in the Moisant School of Aviation at Hempstead, Long Island, in 1911 and was only the second woman in the world to earn her pilot's license. She flew for a time with her school's demonstration team, the Moisant International Aviators. In 1912, wearing a purple silk aviator's costume, she became the first woman to pilot a plane across the English Channel, taking off from Dover, England, and arriving in Hardelot, France, a heroine. That summer she

returned to America to take part in air meets on the East Coast. On July 1, 1912, for reasons that have never been discovered, she lost control of her plane at an air show near Boston. The craft started to roll, and both she and her passenger fell to their deaths.

Mary Lou Retton (1968–)
Gymnast

Mary Lou Retton took her first dance and acrobatics class at age four; at eight she was already a statewide beginners' gymnastics champion in her native West Virginia. A gifted and exuberant athlete, Mary Lou made rapid progress and was competing successfully on an international level by the time she was 13. In 1982 she started training with the renowned gymnastics coach Bela Karolyi. He helped her to refine her style to highlight her incredible strength and compact, muscular body. After just two weeks with Karolyi, Retton earned her first perfect score of ten on the vault.

At the 1984 summer Olympics in Los Angeles, Retton won five medals, including the all-around gold and a silver in the vault—more than any single athlete at the games that year. Her outgoing personality and breathtaking acrobatics made her a favorite with the public. She was named Sportswoman of the Year by *Sports Illustrated* magazine and, the next year, became one of only a handful of female athletes ever to be featured on a Wheaties cereal box. Still extremely popular, Retton continues to endorse products and is a sought-after motivational speaker. She often appears on television as a sports commentator.

Manon Rhéaume (1972–)
Ice hockey goaltender

Manon Rhéaume grew up with two older brothers near Quebec City, in the French-speaking part of Canada. They let her tend goal in their ice hockey games. By the time she was five, she had already played in a local tournament, and she was hooked.

Rhéaume played goalie for boys' teams throughout her school years and went on to play in Canada's

Junior B League, Junior A League, and on the Canadian national women's team. In 1992 she became the first woman ever to play in the all-male National Hockey League (NHL), when she suited up for the Tampa Bay Lightning in a preseason game against the St. Louis Blues, stopping seven of nine shots. The Atlanta Knights, a professional minor-league team, offered her a three-year contract, and she again made history, as the first woman to play in a regular season game. She continues to play on professional minor-league teams with male players. She also helped the Canadian women's team win a silver medal at the 1998 Olympics in Nagano, Japan. Detractors dismiss her presence in the NHL as a publicity stunt, but there is no question Manon can stop a puck. She has kicked open a door for future female players in professional ice hockey.

Wilma Glodean Rudolph (1940–1994)
Sprinter

WILMA RUDOLPH WAS A SICKLY CHILD, WHO suffered double pneumonia, scarlet fever, and—even worse—polio, which caused her left leg to be paralyzed. Despite the doctors' dire predictions,

her family refused to believe she wouldn't improve. The segregated hospitals in their hometown of Clarksville, Tennessee, wouldn't treat an African American, but Wilma's mother drove her 50 miles (80 km) to the nearest integrated hospital for twice-weekly physical therapy. Her brothers and sisters helped by massaging her leg every day. Soon she was on her feet.

By seventh grade Rudolph was playing high school basketball, and in 1956 she became the youngest member of the women's Olympic track team. She won three gold medals at the Rome Olympics in 1960: the 100-meter and 200-meter dashes and the 400-meter relay. The press loved her because of her graceful stride and charming personality, and so, in turn, did fans throughout the world. When she returned to Tennessee, her hometown held a parade in her honor, the first integrated event in Clarksville history.

In 1961 Rudolph received the Sullivan Award for being the country's top amateur athlete, and her career continued impressively. She repeatedly won races in world-record time. She retired in 1962 to raise a family and spent many years teaching and coaching track. In 1981 she founded the Wilma Rudolph Foundation to help young, disadvantaged athletes with their training and education. Her premature death in 1994 was caused by a brain tumor.

Sacagawea (1780s–1812?)
Explorer, guide

ALTHOUGH HER CONTRIBUTION TO THE LEWIS AND Clark expedition was unacknowledged at the time, Sacagawea has since become a legend. Born into the Shoshone tribe of central Idaho, she was captured at age ten by the Hidatsa tribe and taken to their village in what is now North Dakota. She and another Shoshone woman were sold in 1804 to Toussaint Charbonneau, a French-Canadian trapper. Charbonneau made both his wives.

That year Meriwether Lewis and William Clark set out to explore the area between the Mississippi River and the Pacific Ocean. They hired Charbonneau and Sacagawea as interpreters. Carrying her infant son on her back, Sacagawea became vital to the expedition. She acted as an ambassador to the Indians they encountered along the way and showed the travelers how to find edible roots in winter. She helped them

locate her own tribe, the Shoshones, who provided them with badly needed horses and directions. Lewis's diary praises Sacagawea and her bravery highly.

After reaching the Pacific coast, Sacagawea and Charbonneau went back to the Dakota Territory, then moved to St. Louis in 1810. Sacagawea's ultimate fate is uncertain. Charbonneau returned to the Hidatsa village with one—unnamed—wife, who died in 1812. Most historians believe this was Sacagawea. Some accounts say that she stayed in St. Louis, Missouri, with her children, and then moved to a Comanche settlement in Oklahoma. An extremely old woman claiming to be Sacagawea lived among the Wind River Shoshones of Wyoming; she died in 1884.

Eleonora Randolph Sears (1881–1968)
All-around athlete

ELEONORA SEARS, A GREAT-GREAT-GRANDDAUGHTER of Thomas Jefferson, was a member of Boston's social elite. She took advantage of her privileged standing to indulge her unconventional and daring personality. Her financial security made it possible for her to contribute to a variety of worthy sports causes.

Sears—"Eleo" to her friends—played tennis well enough to win the National Women's Doubles Championships four times, and she helped ease tennis' restricted dress code by playing with her sleeves rolled up. She invaded the squash courts at the Harvard Club before women were officially allowed in the building, and eventually popularized the sport for women. She helped found the United States Women's Squash Racquets Association in 1928, won the first U.S. women's singles championship that year, and played until she was 72. She took to long-distance walking, often marching from her Boston home to her summer house 20 miles (32 km) away, or from Boston to Providence, Rhode Island, a distance of about 50 miles (80 km). Every sport thrilled her: polo, sailing, ice skating, golf, and swimming were among her accomplishments.

Her greatest passion, however, was for horses. She bred them, trained them, and rode in equestrian events. She contributed to the United States Equestrian Team and lent them horses for competition. She also provided the financial support to the Boston Mounted Police that prevented the department from being shut down in the late 1950s. Eleonora Sears's exuberance and generosity did not falter until her death from leukemia in 1968.

Tomboy in High Society

Eleonora Sears caused quite a scandal in 1912 when she rode onto a polo field in Burlingame, California, and boldly asked to play on the all-male team. At the time women rode "sidesaddle," with a special saddle that allowed them to sit with both legs on the same side of the horse. But Sears wore trousers and sat astride her horse like a man. The shocked officials refused to let her join the game, of course. And the local Mother's Club issued a public statement asking her to wear "the usual feminine attire." Instead, Eleonora took to appearing in trousers more often.

Mary Decker Slaney (1958–)

Runner

MARY DECKER WAS AN EXCEPTIONAL, ALMOST unbeatable athlete with very bad luck when it came to Olympic competition. She was 11 when, on a lark, she entered her first race near her Los Angeles home and won. By 1972 she was good enough to compete in the Olympics but too young to make the team. She maintained an obsessively rigorous schedule, and at age 15, after setting three world records, she developed crippling shinsplints. The cause was a condition known as compartment syndrome, but it wasn't correctly diagnosed until after the 1976 Olympics.

Decker's hopes for the 1980 Olympics were dashed when America boycotted the games, but she went on to run better than ever. She had an astonishing winning streak in the early 1980s. In 1982 she set seven world records for distances between 800 meters and 10,000 meters and became the first woman to receive the Jesse Owens Award for outstanding track-and-field athlete. She finally made it to the Olympics in 1984 and competed in the 3,000-meter race, during which she was accidentally tripped by her chief rival, South African Zola Budd. Although she set several world records in 1985—the year she married British athlete Richard Slaney—she failed to place at the 1988 Olympics and did not qualify for the 1992 team. She staged an impressive comeback and competed in the 1996 games but did not medal.

Lady Hester Lucy Stanhope (1776–1839)

Traveler

TO SAY THAT LADY HESTER STANHOPE LIVED AN eccentric life is putting it mildly. The daughter of an earl, she spent most of her 20s running the busy household of her uncle and England's prime minister, William Pitt. After his death, the vivacious, restless, and wealthy young woman began a search for another influential position to fill. In 1810 she set out for Constantinople (now Istanbul), intending to obtain a French passport

there and then travel to France to meet Napoleon. However, that plan backfired, so she headed onward, farther into the Middle East.

After she lost all her possessions in a shipwreck, she took to wearing Turkish men's clothes. She spent the next years traveling (for her health, she said) with several companions, including a doctor, her maid, and a few devoted suitors. She charmed the desert people of Syria and Lebanon, who were astonished to see a white woman riding a fast horse and wearing men's clothes. In 1813 she was the first western woman to enter the forbidden city of Palmyra, where it is said that the natives crowned her Queen of the Desert. She settled down in Dar Djoun, an old monastery in the foothills of Mount Lebanon, spent her money lavishly, and dabbled in astrology, which earned her a reputation among the locals as a seer. Gradually, as her behavior became more erratic, her servants and European friends left, and the British government withdrew her pension to pay outstanding debts back home. She died impoverished and was buried at Dar Djoun.

Mabel Stark (1892–?)
Lion tamer

AMERICAN MABEL STARK WAS STUDYING TO BE A nurse when her passion for the circus overcame her desire to work in medicine. She decided to become a large cat tamer because there were no other women in the field.

Stark's act, which included 12 (and sometimes 16) tigers, was soon making headlines. Audiences gasped as she wrestled with them fearlessly and put her head inside their mouths. She always approached the animals with tenderness, never using whips or guns, but her scarred body was living proof that lions and tigers can be trained but not tamed. Once, while performing on a rainy day in 1928, she slipped in the mud and was pounced on by two of the big cats. They mangled one of her legs and nearly severed her jugular vein, but they did not end her career. She went on to write an autobiographical book, *Hold That Tiger* (1938), and continued to appear as a lion and tiger tamer even when she was in her 70s.

Dorothy Dyne Steel (1884–1965)
Croquet player

CROQUET HAS LONG BEEN CONSIDERED SOCIALLY acceptable for women, and they have played for generations. A game of skill and coordination, as opposed to physical strength, it involves using a mallet to hit a wooden ball through wire loops, or wickets, according to a set plan. Many women have excelled at it. But no one has dominated the sport like Englishwoman D. D. Steel did during her career.

Steel won 31 titles—in both women's and men's tournaments—between 1919 and 1939. She was one of only three women ever to win the Open Croquet Championship, and she did so four times, in 1925, 1933, 1935, and 1936. She won the women's championship 15 times. Her handicap, a minus five, was the lowest ever achieved by a woman. Steel was known for her unusual stance and the ease of her strokes; she stood bolt upright, with her heels together and toes apart, then struck the ball with deadly accuracy.

Picabo Street (1971–)
Skier

PICABO STREET GREW UP IN IDAHO, A FREE SPIRIT in a family that encouraged self-expression. She started skiing at age five. By her senior year in high school, she was on the United States Ski Team and had won almost every junior national race. She had also gained a reputation as a "party girl." In 1990 her coach even kicked her off the team for having a bad attitude and being out of shape. However, with her father's help, she got back on track and rejoined the team the next year.

Street won a silver medal in the 1994 Olympics in Norway and, with her colorful, rambunctious personality, became an international favorite. In 1995 she was the first American woman to earn the World Cup downhill title by winning six of nine races in the World Cup circuit; in 1996 she won

the title again. The following year Street suffered a knee injury that required extensive surgery and kept her off skis for several months. Luckily, it didn't deter her from winning the gold medal in the Super-G event at the 1998 Olympic games in Nagano, Japan.

Patricia Head Summitt (1952–)
Basketball coach

BEFORE SHE BECAME ONE OF THE GREATEST COLLEGE basketball coaches in America, Pat Head Summitt was an accomplished player. She attended college in her home state, at the University of Tennessee at Martin, where she set several records. In 1976 she played on the second-place United States Olympic team and the U.S. team that won the Pan American games.

She started coaching women's basketball at the University of Tennessee, Knoxville, in 1974 and has been there ever since. Under her leadership, the UT Lady Volunteers have won six NCAA national championships—in 1987, 1989, 1991, and from 1996 through 1998. In 1977 she coached the U.S. Junior National Team, leading them to two international gold medals, and she served as head coach of the gold medal-winning women's Olympic basketball team in 1984. In 1990 she not only became the first woman to receive the prestigious John Bunn Award for excellence in coaching, she was inducted into the International Women's Sports Hall of Fame.

Summitt has been credited with transforming women's basketball from a careful and predictable game into an exciting and aggressive sport that spectators throng to see. As one of the most successful coaches in the NCAA, she is a prime example of what women can do when they assume leadership positions in sports.

Tabei Junko (1939–)
Mountaineer

JUST AFTER TABEI JUNKO BECAME THE FIRST WOMAN to scale Mount Everest in 1975, she modestly told reporters that she thought of herself as "just a housewife" who loved climbing. She was married with a three-year-old daughter. But the tiny, self-effacing woman from the Fukushima Prefecture in Japan was already a prominent figure in mountaineering, too. She had founded the Japanese Ladies Climbing Club in 1969 and climbed the Himalayan peak Annapurna III the following year.

The expedition to conquer Everest was carried out by an all-female team, and Tabei was the deputy leader. Midway through the climb, they were hit by an avalanche. Several people, including Tabei, were injured, and some of their equipment was lost. Nevertheless, she pushed on. Tabei and Ang Tzering, a male Sherpa guide, were the only members of the expedition to reach the 29,028-foot (8,850-m) summit. Since that time, Tabei has climbed the highest summits on every continent and is active with the Himalayan Adventure Trust of Japan, a group that works to conserve mountain environments.

Valentina Tereshkova (1937–)
Cosmonaut

VALENTINA TERESHKOVA WAS A COTTON MILL worker and an active member of the Soviet Communist party in the city of Yaroslavl when she took up parachuting as a hobby. A naturally athletic woman, she soon became proficient at it and founded the Textile Mill Workers Parachute Club.

In 1961, inspired by cosmonaut Yuri Gagarin's historic first-time orbit of the Earth, Tereshkova wrote a letter to the Soviet space center in Moscow, volunteering to become a cosmonaut. Moscow replied by inviting her to join the cosmonaut training unit the following year.

Tereshkova and a few other women underwent extensive instruction in such required skills as aeronautics, isolation, and spacecraft control, and they were subjected to the same rigorous testing as the men. Then, on June 16, 1963, Tereshkova was launched into orbit on board the *Vostok VI*. She was the first woman in space.

Traveling alone in her space capsule, Tereshkova orbited the planet 48 times during the next three days, then reentered the Earth's atmosphere and parachuted to the ground, a national and international heroine. She graduated from the Zhukovsky Military Air Academy in 1969 with a degree in aerospace engineering and went on to become active in Soviet politics.

Alexandrine Tinné (1835–1869)
Explorer

ALEXANDRINE (ALEXINE, TO HER FAMILY) TINNÉ, was born an heiress to a great fortune in The Hague, Netherlands. Although her early life centered on social obligations and activities, she was always interested in geography. At age 19, she experienced a failed romance with a count. Crushed, she set off on a grand tour of Europe and Egypt with her mother, and her spirits were soon restored. The women spent some time socializing—and in Alexine's case, learning Arabic—in Alexandria and Cairo. Then they traveled along the Nile and across land by camel to the Red Sea.

Tinné was so captivated by Africa that she returned several times, becoming one of only a handful of westerners to explore the Nile and its tributaries. Her fourth trip, which included her mother, her aunt, an ornithologist (bird expert), a botanist (plant expert), six servants, 71 soldiers, and provisions for half a year, was plagued by natural disasters and hostile confrontations. Five people, including Tinné's mother and aunt, died of fever. However, Tinné continued on, along the way collecting many valuable botanical specimens and writing a book,

Plantae Tinneanae (1867), in which she chronicled the expedition and illustrated some of the plants she found. In 1869 she set off to become the first woman to cross the Sahara but was murdered along the way by a gang of bandits from the nomadic Tuareg tribe. She was 34 years old.

Jayne Torvill (1957–)
Pairs ice dancer

JAYNE TORVILL BEGAN SKATING AT AGE TEN IN HER hometown of Nottingham, England, and was soon winning national titles. She became partners with Christopher Dean in 1975. They won their first of six British championship ice-dance titles three years later. From 1981 through 1984, they dominated both the European and the world championships, relinquishing only the 1983 European title, for which they couldn't compete because of an injury to Torvill's shoulder. They took the 1984 Sarajevo Olympics by storm, receiving the highest score possible—a six—19 times. After 1985 Torvill and Dean skated professionally in their own ice show, although they returned to Olympic competition in 1994 to win a bronze medal at Lillehammer, Norway.

Jayne Torvill with her partner, Christopher Dean

Ice dancing often involves projecting a romantic image in performance, so there have always been rumors that Torvill and Dean were a couple. In reality they have a solid working relationship. Jayne Torvill has been married to Phil Christensen since 1990. Torvill and Dean have revolutionized their sport and attracted thousands of devoted fans with their bold, innovative choreography and their ability to create drama together on the ice.

Wyomia Tyus (1945–)
Track-and-field athlete

WHEN GEORGIA NATIVE WYOMIA TYUS received an athletic scholarship to Tennessee State University, she joined the TSU Tigerbelles, a team that produced some of the best female track-and-field athletes of the 1960s. Within a year she was on her way to Tokyo for the 1964 Olympic Games. As a newcomer, she wasn't expected to win, but she tied the 100-meter dash record and earned a gold medal.

Tyus returned to the Olympics in Mexico City in 1968, a time when racial tensions were high in the United States. There she became the first runner ever to win the 100-meter dash in two consecutive Olympics and set a world record in the process. She also won a gold with the 4x100-meter relay team. She dedicated her medals to two male sprinters who were ejected from the Olympics for staging a demonstration protesting America's treatment of black athletes.

In 1969 Tyus gave up her amateur status, but she returned to competition four years later as a professional. She was undefeated in 1975, and her popularity brought well-deserved recognition to her sport and black female athletes. Tyus helped found the Women's Sports Foundation, coached high school track in Los Angeles, California, and became an outspoken defender of civil rights. She was inducted into the National Track and Field Hall of Fame in 1980 and the International Women's Sports Hall of Fame in 1981.

Grete Andersen Waitz (1953–)
Marathon runner

AS A YOUNG RUNNER, GRETE ANDERSEN ACHIEVED a good measure of success running middle distances; at age 16 she won the Norwegian national junior championship in the 400- and 800- meter races. Then in 1978 her husband of

> "I have always loved competition. As a little girl, I would pit myself against a bus or car and try to outrun it. Or when I was given chores to do, I would time myself, seeing how fast I could run to the grocery store and back. As children, we used to play cops and robbers, and it was from this game that I sensed for the first time that I had some running ability. When I was a robber, no one wanted to be the cop to chase me."
>
> **GRETE WAITZ**
> *World Class*, 1986

three years, Jack Waitz, suggested that she enter the New York City Marathon, because he had noticed that Grete excelled at longer distances. She had never run more than 12 miles (20 km) at a time before, but she decided to give it a try. She was not only the first woman across the finish line, she also did it in 2 hours and 32 minutes—a women's world record.

Waitz went on to win the women's title at nine New York City Marathons and several other marathon events all over the world. In 1979 she became the first woman to run a marathon in less than two and a half hours, shaving almost five minutes off her own best time. In 1991, the year of her retirement, she was named best female distance runner of the past 25 years by *Runner's World* magazine. Waitz continues to promote her sport and work as a trainer. She published a book, *On the Run: Exercise and Fitness for Busy People*, in 1997.

Paula Weishoff (1962–)
Volleyball player

CALIFORNIA NATIVE PAULA WEISHOFF WAS SIX feet (1.8 m) tall by the time she was in the eighth grade. She started playing volleyball during her freshman year in high school and three years later was named player of the year in her division. At the University of Southern California, a freshman Weishoff led her college team to the national championship. She quit USC to join the United States national team, and by 1984 she and her teammates had won the silver medal at the Olympics, with Weishoff earning the Most Valuable Player award.

Eager to earn her living playing volleyball, Weishoff joined the women's professional league in Europe and settled happily in Italy. When rules prohibiting professional players from competing in the Olympics changed, she commuted between San Diego and Milan to train for the 1992 games. That summer Team USA took the bronze medal, and Paula was named Outstanding Player. She returned to professional play in Europe, Brazil, and Japan. In 1996 she was the oldest and most experienced member of the U.S. Olympic team, which failed to medal. After retiring from competition, Weishoff returned to USC to coach the women's volleyball team.

Joyce Wethered (1901–1997)
Golfer

JOYCE WETHERED GREW UP IN COUNTY SURREY, England, and inherited her love of golfing from her family. She was also extremely shy and was therefore dismayed to find herself, at the age of 19, the center of national attention when she defeated world-renowned women's champion Cecil Leitch in an amateur tournament.

All together, Wethered won four British Open and five English Ladies' titles. Because she was mobbed by reporters every time she teed off, she retired from competition in 1926. She returned to the spotlight briefly to participate in the 1929 British Open at St. Andrews in Scotland, one of the world's most challenging courses. Wethered won the close, legendary final match against American Glenna Collett, sending the gathered crowds into joyful hysteria.

Sports historians consider Wethered, with her incredible focus and ability to remain calm under pressure, one of the greatest golfers of all time. Joyce herself, however, preferred the quiet life of an English lady. She golfed occasionally as part of a team with her husband, Sir John Heathcoat-Amory, and devoted herself to gardening in her later years.

Winning Ways

One quality that sets a top athlete apart is psychological rather than physical: It is the ability to concentrate fully on the challenge at hand. Golfer Joyce Wethered possessed that talent in abundance. During her first championship tournament, Wethered came from behind and took a small lead. As she prepared for her final putt, a noisy freight train passed nearby, but Wethered didn't even look up. Her putt went in, and the victory was hers. She could have waited for the train to pass before making her play, but when that fact was pointed out to her later she asked, "What train?"

Esther Williams (1923–)
Swimmer, movie star

ESTHER WILLIAMS, ONE OF HOLLYWOOD'S brightest stars in the 1940s and 1950s, glamorized swimming and inspired generations of girls to take to the sport. As a child, Williams counted towels in the locker room of her Los Angeles neighborhood pool in exchange for time in the water. In 1939 she won every race she entered in the Women's Outdoor Swimming Nationals, including the 100-meter freestyle, the 300- and 800-yard relays, and the 100-meter breaststroke, in which she set a national record. If the games hadn't been canceled because of World War II, she would have competed at the Olympics in 1940. Instead, she took a job modeling sportswear in a department store. Later that year she auditioned for a traveling swimming show, Billy Rose's San Francisco Aquacade.

Williams was cast as the lead alongside Olympic champion Johnny Weissmuller, who was already famous for his starring role in *Tarzan* films. When the Aquacade folded in 1941, Williams signed a contract with Hollywood's Metro-Goldwyn-Mayer, even though by her own admission she had no acting, singing, or dancing ability. She made many popular films, including *Bathing Beauty* (1944) and *Million Dollar Mermaid* (1952), which highlighted her grace in the water and her good looks—instead of her acting. After her retirement she turned her attention to the profitable sportswear and equipment companies that bear her name.

May Wirth (1895?–1978)
Equestrian acrobat

BORN IN AUSTRALIA AND ORPHANED AS A VERY young child, May was taken in by the Wirths, a famous performing family. By the age of five, she was a contortionist for the Wirth Brothers Circus.

Maricles Wirth Martin, May's adoptive mother, taught her to ride bareback and to perform stunts, and in 1912 she moved to the United States to join the Barnum & Bailey Circus, where she made her American debut to rave reviews. May performed incredible feats of skill and daring with ease, such as complicated forward and backward somersaults and twists that propelled her from the back of one horse to another, while the animals galloped in wide circles. In 1913 she was seriously injured when she slipped and was dragged around the ring by a frightened horse. However, she returned to the big top the following year. She married a fellow performer, Frank White, in 1919 and continued to be one of the circus' most beloved personalities for another two decades.

Dorothy Wise (1914–1995)
Billiards player

WHEN DOROTHY WISE STARTED SHOOTING POOL in her native Spokane, Washington, there were few national tournaments open to women. Wise had a gift for billiards, however, and she sought out whatever competition she could find, including every local hotshot and tournament that came along. She earned a widespread reputation for being nearly unbeatable and proclaimed herself the unofficial women's champion.

Finally, in the late 1960s, she was given the chance to prove her claim. In 1967 the Billiard Congress of America held its first U.S. Open for women. The 52-year-old Wise won it that year, and for the next four years running. She told reporters that her chance to compete "almost came too late. In pocket billiards the important things are the eyes, nerves, and leg muscles. I swim and ride a bike every day for the leg muscles, but I can't do much about the eyes and the nerves." She was the first woman inducted into the Billiard Congress's Hall of Fame in 1981.

Katarina Witt (1965–)
Figure skater

KATARINA WITT HAS ALWAYS FELT LUCKY TO HAVE grown up in communist East Germany, where the high cost of training world-class athletes—something her family could never have afforded—was subsidized by the government. To Witt, skating is not just a sport but a form of artistic self-expression. She is best known, and loved, for her flirtatious manner and elegance on the ice.

The world was introduced to Witt's style of skating at the 1984 Olympic Games in Sarajevo, where she won the gold medal by one-tenth of a point. In 1988, at the Calgary Olympics, she earned the gold again, becoming the first figure skater since Sonja Henie to win back-to-back Olympic competitions.

By the end of the year, Witt had two world championships and six European championships under her belt, in addition to the Olympic victories. She gave up her amateur status to star in a touring ice show with champion skater Brian Boitano. When the Olympic rules forbidding professional skaters to compete were relaxed in 1994, Witt returned to competition. By then she was considered "past her prime," but she declared that she would continue to skate as long as the public enjoyed her performances. She finished seventh and, as always, delighted her audiences. Witt still appears in many professional exhibitions and competitions.

Hillary Wolf (1978–)
Judo champion

IN HER TEENS, HILLARY WOLF SUCCESSFULLY managed two unrelated careers while still attending high school in Chicago. As an actor, she appeared in ten Hollywood films—among them *Home Alone* (1991) and *Home Alone II* (1992)—by the time she was 15. As an athlete, she trained in judo and became the United States national champion in her weight class. When it came time to choose between the two, Hillary did not hesitate. She chose judo.

Wolf was first introduced to the sport at age seven when, hopelessly bored with studying ballet, she tagged along to her older brother's judo classes. Her natural talent and a strong competitive drive were immediately apparent, so she started training. She was the U.S. national junior judo champion four times before taking the world junior title in the extra lightweight division in 1995. She was the first American to win a world judo championship gold medal. In 1996 Wolf made it to the quarterfinals at the Olympics in Atlanta, but failed to medal. She continues to compete internationally as a martial artist.

Sharon Wood (1957–)
Mountaineer

BORN IN HALIFAX, NOVA SCOTIA, SHARON WOOD fell in love with climbing as a teenager because, she said, it challenged both her body and her mind. She worked as a mountain guide and climbing instructor in the Canadian Rockies after graduating from high school and scaled several of the world's tallest peaks, including Mount McKinley in Alaska and Makalu in the Nepalese Himalayas. Her success won her a position on the Canadian Everest Light Expedition in 1986.

The 13-person Canadian team that traveled to the Himalayas to conquer Everest went without Sherpa guides and carried all their own gear. Along the way they fought viral infections, a four-day storm, and oxygen deficiency. They wanted to reserve their oxygen tanks for the final 12-hour ascent to the summit. When the time came, they distributed the tanks to the two members of the group who were most physically able to go the full distance. One of those two was Wood, who became the first North American woman to reach the top of Mount Everest on May 26, 1986. The following year Wood was awarded the Tenzing Norgay Trophy for her achievement in this male-dominated sport. She continues to climb, and she works as a helicopter ski guide and a motivational speaker.

Lynette Woodard (1959–)
Basketball player

LYNETTE WOODARD TAKES GREAT JOY IN PLAYING basketball. This African American from Wichita, Kansas, averaged 26.3 points per game—a women's NCAA record—as a college player at the University of Kansas at Lawrence. She also kept up a high grade point average as a speech communications major, and she went on to pursue a master's degree after graduating in 1981.

Woodard was a part of the winning Team USA at the Pan American Games in 1983, and she captained the gold medal-winning U.S. Olympic team of 1984. The following year she signed a contract with the Harlem Globetrotters, a comic exhibition team. As the first female member of the Globetrotters, she fulfilled her dream of playing professionally in the United States, where there were few career opportunities for women athletes. Woodard's fun-loving personality and exceptional ball-handling skills fit right in with the team. However, she quit in 1987 because of a disagreement over her contract. She played on several Italian and Japanese basketball teams before becoming a stockbroker at a New York City financial firm.

When the Women's National Basketball Association was established, Woodard jumped at the chance to return to professional basketball. Since 1997 she has played in the WNBA for the Cleveland Rockers.

Fanny Bullock Workman (1859–1925)
Explorer, mountaineer

THE DAUGHTER OF A MASSACHUSETTS GOVERNOR, Fanny Bullock was educated in New York City, Paris, and Dresden, Germany. In 1881 she married a physician, William Workman, from her hometown of Worcester.

Health problems forced William to close his practice, but he was not an invalid for long. The couple led an active life. They began traveling in earnest in 1889 and ended up bicycling, climbing, and exploring together for 25 years. Their first adventure

was a bicycle tour of North Africa, Spain, India, Burma, Cochin China (now Vietnam), and Sri Lanka. However, the Workmans are most famous for their seven mountaineering expeditions into the Karakoram Range, a northern extension of the Himalayas. A determined and aggressive mountaineer, Fanny explored, photographed, and mapped uncharted territory. While her rival, Annie Smith Peck, was setting altitude records in South America, Fanny set records in the East. In 1903 she climbed 21,000 feet (6,401 m), the highest point a woman had ever reached; three years later she beat her own record, reaching 23,300 feet (7,102 m) on the peak of Nun Kun in Kashmir.

The Workmans coauthored a number of books, including *Sketches Awheel in Modern Iberia* (1897), *Peaks and Glaciers of Nun Kun* (1909), and *Two Summers in the Ice-Wilds of Eastern Karakoram* (1917). Fanny also contributed to magazines, was a member of the Royal Geographic Society, and was apparently the first American woman to lecture at the Sorbonne in Paris. She and her husband eventually retired to Cannes, France, where Fanny died at the age of 66.

Kristi Yamaguchi (1971–)
Figure skater

JAPANESE AMERICAN SKATER KRISTI YAMAGUCHI spent her first year of life in plaster casts designed to correct a deformity that caused her feet to curve inward. Perhaps, because she learned to walk balanced on plaster, skates did not feel foreign to her when she strapped them on a few years later.

Yamaguchi took her first lessons at a shopping mall near her California home when she was six. From then on, she dreamed of being a champion. She skated six hours a day and studied with private tutors until her junior year in high school. Kristi competed successfully as a pairs skater in the 1980s, but in 1990 she decided to focus on singles competition. In 1991 she won the world championship and earned her first "six"—a perfect score—for artistic expression. The next year she won the U.S. national title, the gold medal at the Olympics in Albertville, France, her second world championship title, *and* turned professional. She

has been busy ever since, touring with ice shows and doing product endorsements. She is a popular figure in general, but she is a heroine to Asian Americans, a minority group that typically receives little recognition for their athletics.

Mildred "Babe" Didrikson Zaharias (1911–1956)
All-around athlete, golfer

TEXAS NATIVE BABE DIDRIKSON ZAHARIAS WANTED to become "the greatest athlete that ever lived" and pursued that ambition with her own special brand of wisecracking self-confidence and supreme determination. She excelled at every sport she tried, including tennis, basketball, baseball, bowling, track, and golf.

Born Mildred Didrikson, the daughter of Norwegian immigrants, she received her nickname from childhood playmates, who thought her athletic skill resembled that of baseball player Babe Ruth. A basketball star in high school, she was hired to work for the Employers Casualty Company so that she could play on their semiprofessional team in the early 1930s. She entered—and won—the 1932 Amateur Athletic Union women's track-and-field tournament, competing as an individual and outscoring whole teams of athletes. She also earned three Olympic medals that year, taking first place and setting world records in the javelin throw and 80-meter hurdles, and winning a silver medal in the high jump.

In 1935 Didrikson took up golf and was soon ranked number one in the country. She met her husband, the wrestler George Zaharias, at a tournament in 1938; they married later that year. Babe went on to win scores of golfing titles, including the U.S. Open and the British women's amateur championship. In 1946 she helped found the Ladies Professional Golf Association (LPGA), and she was named the Associated Press's Woman Athlete of the Half-Century in 1950.

After undergoing cancer surgery in 1952, Babe came back to win her third women's U.S. Open and the All-American Open golf titles in 1954. The disease returned, however, and she died in 1956, after establishing the Babe Didrikson Zaharias Fund, to finance cancer research.

Galina Zybina (1931–)
Shot-putter

Soviet athlete Galina Zybina almost didn't survive her childhood. She was a girl when World War II ravaged Europe, and her family in Leningrad (now St. Petersburg) was severely affected. Her mother and brother died from exposure and starvation, and she narrowly escaped the same fate. Zybina was extremely weak and thin by the time peace was declared.

However, she not only regained her strength, she became a remarkable athlete. By the early 1950s, she had already set Soviet track-and-field records in the javelin throw and her strongest event, the shot put. She was favored to win in the 1952 Olympics, and she did just that, breaking her own record with a put of 50 feet, 1.75 inches (15.3 m). She continued to perform impressively for over a decade, bringing home a silver Olympic medal in 1956 and a bronze in 1964. In her prime, between 1952 and 1956, Zybina's skill was unparalleled. She set eight consecutive world records during those years, an accomplishment that has assured her a place in sports history.

TIME LINE

776 B.C.E.
The first Olympic Games are held in Greece. Women are prohibited not only from competing in all events, but also from watching the competitions.

500 B.C.E.
Greek women are trained in athletics and gymnastics to cultivate health and beauty. Women in Ionia take part in boar hunts.

160
Female gladiators fight publicly and privately for Roman entertainment. The sport in which women combat one another in teams or individually against dwarfs are eventually prohibited.

1492
The explorer Christopher Columbus lands on San Salvador, an island in the Bahamas, and claims the New World for the Spanish King Ferdinand.

1496
The first known work about the sport of fly-fishing, written by a British nun named Juliana Berners, is published in an anthology, *The Boke of St. Albans*.

1702
British Queen Anne officially approves horse racing and initiates the idea of the sweepstakes, or racing for a cash prize.

Isabel Godin des Odonais

1769
Isabel Godin des Odonais, a native of Ecuador, becomes the first woman known to have traveled the entire length of the Amazon River. She undertook the perilous journey in order to be reunited with her husband, whom she has not seen in two decades.

1775–1783
The American Revolution. The Declaration of Independence is signed in July 1776.

1789–1799
Revolution in France

1805
Explorers Lewis and Clark hire a French-Canadian guide, Toussaint Charbonneau, to lead them to the Pacific. Charbonneau's wife Sacagawea, a Shoshone Indian, saves the explorers from starvation by showing them which roots and berries are edible and communicating with Native American tribes during their difficult journey.

1810
The earliest recorded women's golf match takes place in the town of Musselburgh, Scotland.

1848
The first Women's Rights Convention is held in Seneca Falls, New York.

1860s
Croquet is the first sport in which men and women compete equally. It is also the first sport where women play out-of-doors. The first women's croquet championship is held in England in 1869.

1861–1865
The Civil War in America

1866
Students at Vassar College form the Resolutes, the first collegiate women's baseball team. Women's baseball will gradually evolve into softball over the years.

1867
New York's Knickerbocker Baseball Club establishes the last Tuesday of every month as "Ladies' Day." Wives, girlfriends, and daughters receive free admission to the game.

71

1877   The Wimbledon Tennis Tournament is established in England, but is only open for men's competition.

Lady Anne Blunt

1878   British explorer and expert on Arabian culture Lady Anne Blunt begins to breed Arabian horses at her farm in Sussex, England, and carefully documents their bloodlines. Over a century later, many of the most prized animals owned by Arabian horse enthusiasts will be descendants of her stock.

1879   Women compete in the U.S. National Archery Competition. It is the first time that women participate in a public competition in America.

1884   Wimbledon holds its earliest singles tennis competition for women.

1887 or 1888   American sharpshooter Annie Oakley visits Berlin, where Kaiser Wilhelm asks her to perform one of her most famous stunts, shooting a cigarette from his mouth. Years later, she remarks, "If my aim had been poorer, I might have averted the Great War."

1889   The "safety" bicycle is patented and introduced in the United States. More than a million Americans, including many women, will be riding the bicycle within four years.

1892   The Royal Geographical Society of England, a distinguished organization that has long excluded women, invites a select group of women explorers— among them Isabella Bird—to join. College women begin playing organized basketball after physical education teacher Senda Berenson of Smith College creates an official set of rules for the women's game.

1894   Australia holds its first national golf championship for women.

1896   Modern Olympic Games are held in Athens, Greece. Women are still banned from competing in the competitions, although a Greek woman, Melpomene, unofficially runs the 40-kilometer marathon.

1900   Nineteen women compete in tennis, golf, and yachting events at the Olympic Games held in Paris.

1907   The first women's bowling leagues are formed in St. Louis, Missouri.

1908   Women's figure skating becomes an Olympic event.

1910   Australian swimmer Annette Kellerman creates a stir when she wears her own design—a one-piece bathing suit—and then goes for a swim in Boston Harbor.

1911   Celebrated American climber Annie Smith Peck climbs to the top of Mount Coropuna in Peru and plants a banner reading "Votes for Women."

1912   Fanny Bullock Workman and her husband explore the largest glacier in the Himalayas, the Siachen glacier.

1914–1918   World War I. British explorer and scholar Gertrude Bell is hired by her government as an adviser because of her expertise in Arabian culture and geography.

1919   The Ringling Brothers Circus merges with the Barnum & Bailey Circus. The center-ring attraction at the time, and for the next decade, is aerial acrobat Lillian Leitzel.

Suzanne Lenglen wins the women's singles championship at Wimbledon. She appears for her match wearing a pleated dress without a petticoat, a dramatic departure from conventional tennis attire.

1920   The 19th Amendment to the United States Constitution grants women the vote. It goes into effect August 26th.

1921   The first all-women's Olympic-style competition, the Jeux Olympiques Féminines du Monde, is held in Paris. It is not associated with the traditional Olympics. Rather, it is established as a reaction against the lack of events open to women.

1922   Field hockey player Constance Applebee helps to found the United States Field Hockey Association in Philadelphia. It is established to create standards of play for women's games in clubs and schools.

The American Athletic Union begins the National Indoor and Outdoor Track Championships for Women.

1923   Dance marathoner Alma Cummings wears out several partners and sets a world record by dancing for 27 hours without interruption.

1924   The first modern winter Olympics are held in Chamonix, France. Norwegian skater Sonja Henie makes her debut in front of an international audience.

1926   British golfer Joyce Wethered has become such a sports superstar that reporters follow her wherever she goes. Irritated by this excessive attention, she decides to retire.

1927   American Floretta McCutcheon defeats the top men's bowler, Jimmy Smith, in an exhibition match in Denver, Colorado.

1928   Eleonora Sears wins the first U.S. national women's squash title

Eleonora Sears

at age 46. She will continue to compete until age 70.

1932   Women's speed skating is held for the first time at the winter Olympics in Lake Placid, New York.

Amelia Earhart becomes the first woman pilot to fly alone across the Atlantic Ocean.

1934   Babe Didrikson, one of the first great all-around women athletes, pitches a whole inning against the Brooklyn Dodgers in an exhibition game for the Philadelphia Athletics.

1937   The first U.S. women's bicycling championship is held in Buffalo, New York. The winner takes 22.4 seconds to finish the one-mile (.6-km) course.

1938   Helen Wills Moody wins the Wimbledon Tournament in ladies' singles tennis for the record-breaking eighth time.

1939   Peruvian bullfighter Conchita Cintrón makes her debut at age 17 in Mexico, where it is legal for women to be *toreras*.

1939–1945   World War II. Two consecutive Olympic Games are canceled because of the conflict.

1942   American professional golfer Patty Berg takes a break from her successful career to serve as a lieutenant in the Marine Corps.

1946	U.S. Ladies Professional Golfers Association (LPGA) is organized.
1948	At the summer Olympic Games in London, Alice Coachman wins the high jump, becoming the first African American woman to bring home gold. Her teammate Audrey Patterson is the first black female medal-winner, having won a bronze in the 200-meter sprint, an earlier event.
1951	American Florence Chadwick is the first woman to swim across the English Channel from England to France.
1953	"Little Mo" Connolly becomes the first woman to win tennis' Grand Slam.
1955	Women's basketball is included in the Pan American Games for the first time.
1957	Marion Ladewig is the first woman to achieve the title of International Bowler of the Year. American tennis player Althea Gibson is the first black woman invited to play at Wimbledon, and she wins the ladies' singles title.
1960	Wilma Rudolph wins three gold medals in track and field at the summer Olympics in Rome. The first Paralympic Games are held. From then on, this event, which is administered by a branch of the International Olympic Committee, takes place approximately two weeks after the Olympic Games in the same city. The Paralympics are not only intended to promote greater public awareness about the capabilities of people with disabilities. They also provide world-class competition for top disabled athletes.
1961	The entire United States figure skating team is killed when their airplane crashes en route to the world championships in Prague, Czechoslovakia. Among the victims

is Billy Kipp, Peggy Fleming's first coach. The tragedy inspires Fleming to train even harder, in Kipp's honor.

1962	Phenomenal American softball pitcher Joan Joyce gives an exhibition with Boston Red Sox star Ted Williams. She pitches more than 30 balls to Williams, but he only manages one feeble hit and a few fouls.
1963	Soviet cosmonaut Valentina Tereshkova becomes the first woman in outer space when she orbits the Earth 48 times in the space capsule *Vostok VI*.
1967	American Margaret Murdock sets a world record in the small-bore rifle competition at the Pan American Games. It is the first time in sports history that a woman has surpassed a men's record.
1968	American runner Wyomia Tyus becomes the first person ever to win two consecutive Olympic sprint titles when she wins her second gold in the 100-meter dash.
1970	Diane Crump is the first woman jockey to ride in the Kentucky Derby. She finishes in 15th place. The first all-women tennis tour is established as the Virginia Slims Tour, sponsored by the Philip Morris cigarette company.
1972	At the Olympic Games in Munich, Palestinian terrorists sneak into the athletes' compound and take 11 Israelis hostage. They kill two immediately, then ask for the release of 200 Arab prisoners. West German negotiators convince the terrorists to leave the compound, but a disastrous shoot-out ensues. All nine Israelis, five of the eight terrorists, and one police officer are killed. Women are officially allowed to enter in the Boston Marathon for the first time since it was established in 1897.

Russian gymnast Olga Korbut is the first person to accomplish a backward somersault on the balance beam.

1973 American Billie Jean King soundly defeats fellow tennis player Bobby Riggs in an exhibition game. Riggs had challenged King to this "Battle of the Sexes," proclaiming that no woman was a match for him.

The U.S. Open is the first major tennis competition to offer equal prize money to the men's and women's singles champions.

1974 The Little League Baseball Organization begins to accept girls on all teams across the country.

1975 Tabei Junko of Japan is the first woman to reach the peak of Mount Everest, the world's tallest mountain.

1976 At the summer Olympic Games, Romanian gymnast Nadia Comaneci not only scores the first perfect ten ever, she repeats the feat six more times, for seven record-breaking scores in all.

1977 New Zealander Naomi James becomes the first woman ever to sail around the world alone.

1978 Englishwoman Clare Francis crosses the Atlantic Ocean in record time for a woman sailing solo.

Clare Francis

1980 The United States boycotts the Summer Olympics, to be held in Moscow as a political protest against the Soviet Union's invasion of Afghanistan. Sixty-one other nations join the boycott.

1983 American Joan Benoit-Samuelson wins her second Boston Marathon and sets a new women's record.

1984 Czech-born tennis star Martina Navratilova wins both the U.S. and British women's singles titles.

1985 Lynette Woodard, basketball star of the University of Kansas, joins the Harlem Globetrotters as their first woman team member.

1986 Susan Butcher wins the Iditarod Trail Dog Sled Race. She will win again in 1988 and 1990.

1987 American basketball player Nancy Lieberman-Cline joins a men's team in the U.S. Basketball League.

1989 German Steffi Graf wins both the British and U.S. Open singles titles at age 20.

The International Women's Sports Hall of Fame is founded.

1991 The first Women's World Cup for Soccer is held in China.

1994 American rock climber Lynn Hill free-climbs the "nose" of a rock called El Capitan in Yosemite, California, an achievement that was previously considered impossible.

1995 In February at the Calgary World Cup, American speed skater Bonnie Blair breaks her own world record, finishing the 500-meter race in just 38.69 seconds.

1998 British ice dancers Jayne Torvill and Christopher Dean collaborate with the cellist Yo-Yo Ma, choreographing a skating routine to accompany Ma's rendition of Johann Sebastian Bach's *Sixth Suite for Unaccompanied Cello.*

GLOSSARY

Amateur: a person who participates in an activity for pleasure rather than for financial gain.

Contortionist: an acrobat whose specialty consists of "contorting," or twisting, his or her body into uncommon positions.

Épée: in fencing, the modern descendant of the dueling sword. An épée has a rigid, tapering blade and no cutting edge.

Final Four: the last leg of the annual NCAA basketball championship tournaments held for both men's and women's college teams. The winning team from each of the four regions of the United States—the South, Midwest, East, and West—goes on to the "Final Four" portion of the tournament and competes for the national title.

Free climb: in rock climbing, when the climber ascends the rock face without using safety harnesses, ropes, or other similar devices.

Freestyle: in swimming, a race or competition in which the racer may use any stroke she or he chooses.

Grand master: an exceptionally skillful chess player, often a title conferred after a player wins an international tournament.

Handicap: in sports, when the better player starts out with a scoring disadvantage, so that she or he can compete evenly against lesser players.

Links: a golf course.

Marathon: a footrace that covers 26 miles, 385 yards (42.2 km). The race was originally approximately 25 miles (40.5 km), but the new distance became standard in 1908 when the Olympic Games took place in London. Queen Alexandra, wife of Edward VII, wanted the race to start in front of Windsor Castle and end at the royal box in the stadium.

NCAA: the National Collegiate Athletic Association. Founded in 1906, it was originally called the Intercollegiate Athletic Association, but the name was changed in 1910. The NCAA represents American colleges and universities. It is a voluntary organization that comprises more than 1,200 institutions, individuals, and organizations devoted to intercollegiate athletics.

Open: in sports such as golf and tennis, a tournament that admits both professionals and amateurs. Also, sometimes, a competition that allows both men and women to enter.

Par: in golf, the number of strokes an experienced player should need to complete a hole or the entire course. A standard round of golf is 18 holes, and par for the course is usually 72 strokes.

Pentathlete: an athlete who competes in pentathlons. The modern-day pentathlon (the word comes from the Greek meaning "five contests") is a grueling sequence of events consisting of swimming, cross-country running, an equestrian race, fencing, and target shooting.

Perfect game: in baseball or softball, a game in which the pitcher prevents the opposing team from hitting, walking, or scoring at all. No player ever even reaches first base.

Platform diving: an event in which dives are performed from a firm, stationary platform that is suspended either ten meters or five meters above the surface of the water.

Professional: in sports, an athlete who is paid to perform or compete for prize money. Many events don't allow professional competitors or set limits on the income they are allowed to earn if they do participate.

Relay race: a team race in sports such as swimming or track, in which the course is divided into several parts, or legs. Each leg is traveled by a different athlete, and no racer may start until the preceding teammate has completed his or her segment.

Seeded: ranked relative to the skill levels of all the players in a tournament. It is also called "seeding" when a tournament's schedule is arranged so that the top-ranked (top-seeded) athletes do not play against each other in the earliest rounds.

Sherpa: a Tibetan group of people who inhabit the southern slopes of the Himalayas. Because of their familiarity with the terrain, Sherpas are often employed as guides and porters by mountaineers who set out to climb Himalayan peaks.

Shutout: a game in which the opposing team does not score.

Shuttlecock: the object that is struck back and forth over the net in badminton. Designed and balanced to move at high speeds through the air, it has a rounded front end made from rubber or, traditionally, cork, and plastic or feathers projecting behind.

Slalom: A downhill ski race through an obstacle course. The skier is required to zigzag back and forth, encountering and successfully negotiating, each obstacle.

Springboard diving: an event in which the dives are performed from a flexible—springy—board that is suspended either three meters or one meter above the surface of the water.

Super-G: short for "super-giant slalom" in skiing. A race that combines a slalom and a downhill racing course.

Torera: a woman bullfighter.

Triple Crown: in American horse racing, an unofficial title that is awarded when a horse wins the Kentucky Derby, the Belmont Stakes, and the Preakness Stakes all in the same season. Only 11 horses have managed to capture the Triple Crown.

Triple loop: in figure skating, a jump for which the skater must take off from the outer edge of one skate, perform three full rotations (spins) in the air, and then land on the same outer skate edge.

INDEX

Numbers in boldface type indicate main entries.

CREDITS

Quotes

13 Berners, Juliana, Dame. *A Treatise on Fishing with a Hook, attributed to Dame Juliana Berners, printed in the book of Saint Albans by Wynken De Worde, Mcccclxxxxvi, and rendered into Modern English by William van Wyck, Mcmxxxiii.* New York: Van Rees Press, 1933. **26** Francis, Clare. *Come Hell or High Water.* London: Pelham Books, 1977. Used by permission. **31** Hashman, Judy Devlin. *Badminton a Champion's Way.* London: Kaye & Ward, 1969. **37** Kingsley, Mary. *Travels in West Africa.* London: Macmillan & Co. Ltd., 1897. **42** Lieberman, Nancy. *Basketball My Way.* New York: Charles Scribner's Sons, 1982. Used by permission. **52** Murphy, Dervla. *Wheels Within Wheels: Autobiography.* London: John Murray, 1917. Used by permission. **56** Pfeiffer, Ida. *A Lady's Second Journey Around the World.* New York: Harper and Brothers, 1856. **64** Waitz, Grete and Gloria Averbuch. *World Class.* New York: Warner Books, 1986. Used by permission.

Photographs

Abbreviations
AP   AP Wide World Photos
COR   Corbis
HG   Hulton Getty
LOC   Library of Congress

8 Adams, Harriet, LOC; Akeley, Delia, LOC. **11** Balukas, Jean, LOC; Bell, Gertrude, HG. **12** Berg Patricia, HG. **13** Bird, Isabella, LOC. **14** Blanchard, Madeleine, LOC. **15** Blankers-Koen, Fanny, LOC. **16** Brasuhn, Midge, LOC. **17 (and title page)** Bruce, Mildred, HG. **18** Chadwick, Florence, LOC. **19** Cintrón, Conchita, COR/Hulton-Deutsch Collection; Coleman, Bessie, U.S. Post Office. **21** Connolly, Maureen, HG. **22** DeFrantz, Anita, AP. **23 (and cover)** Devers, Gail, COR/Ales Fevzer; Earhart, Amelia, LOC. **24** Elek, Ilona, HG. **25** Fleming, Peggy, HG. **27** Fu Mingxia, AP; **(and 7)** Gibson, Althea, LOC. **29** Graf, Steffi, COR/Dimitri Iundt. **30** Hamm, Mia, AP. **31 (and cover)** Henie, Sonja, HG. **32** James, Naomi, HG. **34** Josephson, Karen and Sarah, AP. **35** Kellerman, Annette, LOC. **36** King, Billie Jean, LOC. **37** Korbut, Olga, HG. **38** Krone, Julie, COR/Jerry Cooke. **39** Latynina, Larissa, LOC. **40** Laumann, Silken, AP. **41 (and 6)** Leitzel, Lillian, LOC; Lenglen, Suzanne, HG. **43** Lobo, Rebecca, AP. **44 (and title page)** McCutcheon, Floretta, LOC. **45** Markham, Beryl, LOC. **46** Menchik-Stevenson, Vera, HG. **47** Mitchell, Jackie, LOC. **48** Mittermaier, Rosi, COR/Bettmann; Moody, Helen Wills, HG. **50** Muldowney, Shirley, National Hot Rod Association. **51** Mullins, Aimee, AP. **52** Navratilova, Martina, Carol L. Newsom Associates. **53 (and title page)** Oakley, Annie, LOC. **54** Ostermeyer, Micheline, LOC. **55 (and cover)** Peck, Annie Smith, LOC. **57** Quimby, Harriet, LOC. **58 (and title page)** Rudolph, Wilma, LOC. **59** Sacagawea, LOC. **60** Stanhope, Hester Lucy, LOC. **61 (and cover)** Street, Picabo, COR/Wally McNamee. **62** Tereshkova, Valentina, HG. **63** Tinné, Alexandrine, LOC. **64** Torvill, Jayne, HG. **66** Williams, Esther, HG; Wirth, May, LOC. **68 (and 6)** Workman, Fanny, LOC. **69** Yamaguchi, Kristi, COR/Neal Preston. **70 (and 7)** Zaharias, Mildred, LOC. **71** Godin des Odonais, Isabel, LOC. **72** Blunt, Lady Anne, LOC. **73** Sears, Eleonora, LOC. **75** Francis, Clare, HG.

SBC